In *The Life You Were Reborn to Live*, Gary Thomas does an exceptional job unpacking common lies that lead us away from freedom into bondage. As we identify these lies and then work to dismantle them, we can walk the path back to freedom. Acknowledging these lies is painful, but the freedom that awaits is worth it.

KYLE IDLEMAN, SENIOR PASTOR, SOUTHEAST CHRISTIAN CHURCH; BESTSELLING AUTHOR OF *EVERY THOUGHT CAPTIVE*

I've said this about Gary Thomas for years: Long after he's gone, his books will be considered classics in the Christian literary world. For as long as I've known (and had the privilege of interviewing) Gary, his greatest passion has been his oneness with God Almighty. A wellspring of wisdom, he perpetually seeks out the deep things of God. He is not content with platitudes and formulas; he searches for biblical truth and the redemptive life Jesus died to give us. In this book, Gary dismantles lies we've walked with, lived with, and seldom considered challenging. But these aren't your everyday lies. Gary explores wrong beliefs that center our Christian life around ourselves and make an idol out of our preferences. Lies in any form hold us captive and prevent us from living free, healed, and whole. If you're ready to shed the lies like an outdated winter coat, let the truths on these pages seep into your soul. A new life-giving season awaits.

SUSIE LARSON, BESTSELLING AUTHOR; TALK RADIO HOST; NATIONAL SPEAKER

I didn't know how much I needed this book. Gary's fresh approach to topics that aren't often broached, combined with his directness and grace, kept me turning the pages. We are in a cultural moment that needs wisdom—this book is aptly timed.

SARA HAGERTY, BESTSELLING AUTHOR, *UNSEEN: THE GIFT OF BEING HIDDEN IN A WORLD THAT LOVES TO BE NOTICED*

Like a map that highlights both well-worn paths and lesser-known trails, *The Life You Were Reborn to Live* invites readers to reexamine their journey of faith. While some may choose different routes than those suggested in this volume, this book serves as a compass for those seeking to navigate the complex terrain of the spiritual life.

FRANK VIOLA (FRANKVIOLA.ORG), AUTHOR OF *THE UNTOLD STORY OF THE NEW TESTAMENT CHURCH* AND *INSURGENCE*

Gary Thomas has written a helpful, wise, and biblically based book on the life we were reborn to live as Christians in intimacy with God. He emphasizes the need for dismantling twelve lies that impede our progress as Christ followers. Highly recommended!

SIANG-YANG TAN, PHD, SENIOR PROFESSOR OF CLINICAL PSYCHOLOGY, FULLER THEOLOGICAL SEMINARY; AUTHOR, *COUNSELING AND PSYCHOTHERAPY*

This insightful, practical, and at times shockingly countercultural book is filled with fresh truth in a time when deceptive spiritual agendas abound and seek to poison our lives. With rich theological depth and accessible language, Gary Thomas leads us on a journey of identifying false narratives and embracing God's vision for those reborn by the power of Jesus.

REV. DR. KEVIN G. HARNEY, FOUNDER AND PRESIDENT, ORGANIC OUTREACH INTERNATIONAL; AUTHOR, THE ORGANIC OUTREACH TRILOGY

Gary Thomas has a heart for God. He writes as one who longs to share with others what he has learned from his years of faithful Scripture study. This book is a masterful critique of the clichés, commonplaces, and even lies we often hear and too easily accept as true. Gary is unafraid to say what Scripture says, to challenge what everyone knows—and to do so with humility and compassion. This book will help those who long to serve Christ and be faithful members of the church. I highly recommend this thoughtful and biblically grounded study of specific and practical ways for each of us to clear our minds and set our feet firmly on the path toward intimacy with God.

ROBERT SLOAN, PRESIDENT, HOUSTON CHRISTIAN UNIVERSITY

# THE LIFE
## YOU
## WERE REBORN
## TO LIVE

# THE LIFE YOU WERE REBORN TO LIVE

*Dismantling 12 Lies*
*That Rob Your*
*Intimacy with God*

## GARY THOMAS

**ZONDERVAN BOOKS**

ZONDERVAN BOOKS

*The Life You Were Reborn to Live*
Copyright © 2025 by The Center for Evangelical Spirituality

Published by Zondervan, 3950 Sparks Drive SE, Suite 101, Grand Rapids, MI 49546, USA. Zondervan is a registered trademark of The Zondervan Corporation, L.L.C., a wholly owned subsidiary of HarperCollins Christian Publishing, Inc.

Requests for information should be addressed to customercare@harpercollins.com.

Zondervan titles may be purchased in bulk for educational, business, fundraising, or sales promotional use. For information, please email SpecialMarkets@Zondervan.com.

ISBN 978-0-310-36068-1 (international trade paper edition)
ISBN 978-0-310-36067-4 (audio)

Library of Congress Cataloging-in-Publication Data

Names: Thomas, Gary (Gary Lee) author
Title: The life you were reborn to live : dismantling 12 lies that rob your intimacy with God / Gary Thomas.
Description: Grand Rapids, Michigan : Zondervan Books, [2025]
Identifiers: LCCN 2025017612 (print) | LCCN 2025017613 (ebook) | ISBN 9780310360650 hardcover | ISBN 9780310360667 ebook
Subjects: LCSH: Christian life—Christianity
Classification: LCC BV4501.3 .T471534 2025 (print) | LCC BV4501.3 (ebook) | DDC 248.4—dc23/eng/20250702
LC record available at https://lccn.loc.gov/2025017612
LC ebook record available at https://lccn.loc.gov/2025017613

HarperCollins Publishers, Macken House, 39/40 Mayor Street Upper, Dublin 1, D01 C9W8, Ireland (https://www.harpercollins.com)

*Cover design: Spencer Fuller / Faceout Studio*
*Cover illustrations: Tartila / Shutterstock*
*Interior design: Mallory Collins*

*Printed in the United States of America*

25 26 27 28 29 LBC 5 4 3 2 1

*To Skip, Robert, Gus, Jim,*
*and occasionally David—*
*a band of brothers*
*in Bible study and prayer since 2010*

# CONTENTS

# CONTENTS

# INTRODUCTION

We've all been told a lot of lies in our lifetime that haunt us, keep us frustrated, and make us value the wrong things, resent the wrong things, and desire the wrong things. Some of them are silly, but think for a moment how widespread they were, how we accepted them without thinking, and how we organized our lives accordingly.

For instance, remember when we were told that margarine was better for us than butter? I recall my mom serving up a product labeled "I Can't Believe It's Not Butter." For the record, *I* could, and nutritionists now know it was far worse for my body than butter.

To this day I'm plagued with a lie from my past. For decades I've been told that to go fastest on my bicycle, I need to pump up my tires to their maximum PSI (pounds per square inch). That's what the pros in the Tour de France did up until about the last decade. But now science tells us that's not true—less inflated tires can go faster (and are less prone to blow out while also gripping the road better). But it still *feels* wrong for me not to inflate my tires up to the max. Why? Because I was told to do that for decades. What feels right isn't always right, even though wrong is always destructive.

Some lies had an agenda. I also remember being told that when you shave your hair, it comes back thicker and darker. As a bald man who has his head shaved once a month, I can attest that this is just not true (though I dearly wish it was). But it's what parents in the prior generation told my generation when they didn't want their daughters to start shaving their legs "too soon."

Whether the lies are intentional or based on ignorance, they are still lies we need to dismantle. We've accepted them, allowed them to shape our actions, and limited our lives accordingly.

## SPIRITUAL LIES WITH AN AGENDA

The Bible warns us about something more sinister going on—*spiritual lies that have an agenda*. They're based not on ignorance but on malice. They are weeds sown into the garden of God's church to lead God's children astray from a flourishing life in Christ. Every lie you hear and believe cuts you off from flourishing in that aspect of life.

Every one.

And many of them are even born, propagated, and defended in some churches. These spiritual lies are far more serious than what kind of spread we put on our toast or how much air we put into our tires. That's why if there's one thing a Christian can't afford to take for granted, it's the truth. What we believe impacts us emotionally, spiritually, relationally, and physically. The apostle Paul wrote, "Do not conform to the pattern of this world, but be transformed by the renewing of your mind" (Romans 12:2).

Every age has its own "pattern." I believe today's age focuses on distraction. The world's agenda is to distract us from delighting in God, cause us to lose our satisfaction in God, ruin our faith in God, and make us miss out on living lives of fulfilling obedience.

When we dismantle the twelve lies we'll talk about in this book, we stop being conformed to the pattern of this world and start being transformed by the renewing of our minds.

Here are the twelve truths we'll focus on in this book:

1. We all want peace, in theory, but true peace awaits those who press into Jesus. Trying to gain peace from our circumstances apart from Jesus will prevent us from finding the restfulness our souls crave. The less we understand what creates inner peace, the more we chase it, and the more we'll keep pushing it away.

2. Letting go of control of our lives may feel scary and even irresponsible, but when we give control to God, we will be directed by him, and he's much better at controlling our lives than we are.

3. Trying to find our ultimate meaning in our family keeps us from loving them as we should while blinding us to the fulfillment of being a part of God's family.

4. Giving up relationships because they can be frustrating and hurtful inhibits us from the satisfaction of living in community.

5. Settling for a salvation that is all about us hinders us from the salvation that swells our souls with purpose, and robs us of the joy of being used by God for his kingdom work.

6. Obsessing over our own comfort blocks us from the refining work of adversity.

7. Wanting to be free of sin now can result in seeking shortcuts, but we will miss out on the wisdom of what our sin and temptations can teach us. It will also rob us of the glory of resting in the work of Jesus' righteousness rather than our own.

8. Being a consumer of the church strips us of the joy and fulfillment of serving the church; it turns us from loving Jesus' bride to resenting an institution because it's not perfect like Jesus.

9. Settling for a materialistic worldview out of embarrassment

keeps us from the wonder of living life with supernatural oversight and assistance.

10. Living a rich-toward-God life is one of the most common themes in the Christian classics. It refers to shaping our hearts toward what truly matters, setting us free from the brutal dogfight of trying to find success, meaning, and fulfillment in this world.

11. If we remain ensconced in an entitlement mentality (perhaps the greatest spiritual trap of our age), we will be mired in bitterness and anger, keeping us from gratitude toward God and a sense of wonder at his goodness.

12. Neglecting to actively cultivate more wisdom is to live in a perpetual twilight that is closer to darkness than dawn; we'll miss out on the true nature of things—the things that truly matter and give lasting satisfaction.

Dismantling the lies behind these truths is an active process. Renewing our minds renews our lives, sets us free from the consequences of lies, and introduces new joy. By rethinking what we take for granted, we can do away with fears and find joy and hope where we used to struggle with bitterness, resentment, and anger. The abundant Christian life, the victorious Christian life, the joy-filled and peace-filled Christian life, is based on truth. Every lie we believe about God changes the way we look at him and respond to him. Just as harmful, when we believe a lie, we'll tend to spread our lies—all with good intentions—and incarcerate our fellow believers in the prisons of our own deceptions.

Dismantling false beliefs is like losing excess weight, getting out of debt, and completing a house remodel all together in one fell swoop. For me, walking through this process felt like walking through a wardrobe into Narnia, opening new spiritual worlds and experiences. Embracing these new truths has mapped out the course to an entirely new life. Just as Lucy invited her siblings to join her in her adventures to Narnia, I invite you to join me in exploring richer and deeper spiritual realities than you might have imagined.

## THE SPIRIT OF THE WORLD IS LIVING FOR LESS

William Law published his seminal work, *A Serious Call to a Devout and Holy Life*, in 1728. His description of the shallow and illusory life that most people seek is startlingly similar to life today:

> To abound in wealth, to have fine houses and rich clothes, to be attended with splendour and equipage [a fancy coach], to be beautiful in our persons, to have titles of dignity, to be above our fellow-creatures, to command the bows and obeisance [respect] of other people, to be looked on with admiration, to overcome our enemies with power, to subdue all that oppose us, to set ourselves in as much splendor as we can, to live highly and magnificently, to eat and drink and delight ourselves in the most costly manner— these are the great, the honourable, the desirable things, to which the spirit of the world turns the eyes of all people. And many a man is afraid of . . . not engaging in the pursuit of these things, lest the same world should take him for a fool.[1]

Over the past three hundred years, the "spirit of the world" hasn't changed much, has it? Even though this is the road to spiritual ruin, people today essentially seek the same things they ran after in the eighteenth century. We may travel in cars and planes instead of coaches, but we still want power, comfort, affluence, public acclaim, and people who will envy us, at least a little. We want to be at least mildly attractive and increasingly look younger than we really are. We don't want to be anonymous or ignored. We're not concerned about whether we have two or four horses pulling our buggy, but we do get to decide between a luxury SUV and a used sedan.

The challenge, according to Law, is that "the history of the Gospel is chiefly the history of Christ's conquest over this spirit of the world. And the number of true Christians is only the number of those who, following the spirit of Christ, have lived contrary to this spirit of the world."[2]

Living the Christian life calls us to identify and then reject the false agenda of our age: "Do not conform to the pattern of this world." *Our daily choices proclaim either the victory of Christ in our lives or our surrender to this age.* With values radically at odds with each other, every inch you incline toward the world is an inch you are crawling away from Christ.

The problem is that even many Christians don't understand how the lies of this age are designed to distract us from the truth of Christ. Life in Christ is thus a "thinking life" because the power of the world is built upon a blind obedience to it. William Law writes these words:

> A devout man makes a true use of his reason; he sees through the vanity of the world, discovers the corruption of his nature and the blindness of his passions. He lives by a law which is not visible to vulgar eyes; he enters into the world of spirits; he compares the greatest things, sets eternity against time, and chooses rather to be for ever great in the presence of God, when he dies, than to have the greatest share of worldly pleasures whilst he lives.[3]

Life in Christ flourishes when we keep thinking differently than the way the world thinks, valuing different things, pursuing different things, and seeking to please an entirely different audience. The apostle John put it this way: "They are from the world and therefore speak from the viewpoint of the world, and the world listens to them. We are from God, and whoever knows God listens to us; but whoever is not from God does not listen to us" (1 John 4:5–6).

As it is when I go to fill my bicycle tires, the challenge is that if we've always done something because we think it's the thing we're supposed to do, it feels wrong to do it differently, even though it's right. It's not always easy to unlearn "wrong," especially when we're convinced wrong is right. But it's vital to make this mental shift. It feels right to build a life that's comfortable in the world, even though Scripture calls it wrong: "Since, then, you have been raised with Christ, set your hearts on things above, where Christ is, seated at the right hand of God. Set your minds on things above, not on earthly things. For you died, and your life is now hidden with Christ in God" (Colossians 3:1–3).

I'm hopeless with directions—especially when it comes to one particular exit off the Denver toll road where I'm supposed to take the north exit toward Denver, even though I live south of Denver. Lisa, my wife, is great with directions, and she will patiently tell me, "No, stay right," even though going right feels wrong to me. In the same way, the apostle Paul told us, "Do not conform to the pattern of this world, but be transformed by the renewing of your mind" (Romans 12:2).

The NIV's use of the word *world* to translate the Greek word *aion* may be deceiving to some. *Aion* is often better translated as "age." It's Paul's way of saying we live in the new era with a new mindset and a new understanding. Every age has its own agenda; our mission is to challenge the premises of this age's agenda, compare it to God's, reject what is false in this world, and embrace what is true in the Spirit.

How we think is how we will live. Paul doubled down on this in Ephesians. Putting off the old self (4:22) and putting on the new self (v. 24) centers around being "made new in the attitude of your minds" (v. 23). We must unlearn what we thought before, relearn (or learn for the first time) God's revolutionary truth, and then and *only* then can we "put on the new self, created to be like God in true righteousness and holiness" (v. 24). Paul proceeded in the following verses to tell the Ephesians how to behave, beginning with, "Each of you must put off falsehood and speak truthfully" (v. 25).

We must dismantle the lies we've believed before we can be made new. If we accept the premise of a lie, we'll pursue that lie and in the end be ruined by it.

Karl Barth, the renowned twentieth-century Swiss theologian, paints a helpful patina over Romans 12:2, translating it as follows: "I beseech you—not to fashion yourselves according to the present form of this world, but according to its coming transformation."[4] This monumental statement is a clear call to base our lives on the world's *coming transformation* rather than the passing *fashion* of this world. Paul's invitation is phenomenal: It's a new age, and you are a new person. Believe and live like it.

Two of my children had the great blessing of attending a public high school led by a principal (Steve Clark) who was a finalist for the National Principal of the Year award. Our city had three high schools, but parents were begging to get their kids into the one Steve oversaw. Early in the school year, when a couple of transfer students got into a fistfight, Steve brought them to his office and said, "Maybe you don't understand, but fighting isn't how we settle things here at Bellingham High School."

*This is a new place; we operate by different rules.*

And with that thinking, Steve created a flourishing place for students to learn. The two students had learned to survive in their old school by fighting. But they were in a new school now and needed to unlearn that strategy. There was a different way to live.

The twelve truths we'll talk about in this book represent twelve different mindsets and ways to live.

## EXPOSING THE GREAT ILLUSION

John the Baptist (Matthew 3:1–2) and Jesus (4:17) both began their public ministries with a focus on repentance. The first key component of repentance is *rethinking* (what I'm calling *dismantling*). This age's agenda to trap us in distractions has grown stronger, not weaker. Would you care to join me in protesting against this great illusion instead of being spellbound by it? Will you unlearn what isn't true and embrace a more exalted life as a citizen of God's kingdom?

When we unmask the lies that not only seek to conform us but also keep us captive, we can attain the glory that is rightfully ours in Christ. There is an utterly captivating, glorious, powerful, reassuring, and supernaturally peaceful new spiritual life waiting for you. You just have to leave the old life first.

At times throughout my life, I have fallen captive to lies the world repeats to me over and over until I assume the lies must be true. Other times, frankly, I've been held back by lies I've heard in church. The dismantling we're talking about must take place in all sectors, but the gist is this: To get to the promised land, we must first leave Egypt.

New Testament scholar John Stott pointed out that "do not conform" is a repeated pattern of instruction throughout Scripture.[5] Leviticus 18:3 reads, "You must not do as they do in Egypt, where you used to live, and you must not do as they do in the land of Canaan, where I am bringing you. Do not follow their practices." Jesus describes to his followers the practices of the Pharisees and pagans and says, "Do not be like them" (Matthew 6:8).

To live in the new era of life in Christ, we must unmask, dismantle, and discard (repent of) the old deceptions that formerly captivated our hearts and minds—sometimes those that are of the world, sometimes those that are of organized religion. This is a radical call to become committed nonconformists. We must say no to the great illusion in order to say yes to God's glorious truth. We must choose sides. Paul said in Galatians 1:4 that Jesus "gave himself for our sins to *rescue us* from the present evil age" (emphasis added). If his aim is to rescue us from this present evil age, we can't espouse it, believe it, or chase after it—even though many Christians do. We *must* leave it.

The coming of Christ signals the end of the present age: "The world and its desires pass away, but whoever does the will of God lives forever" (1 John 2:17). How do we know God's will? The second half of Romans 12:2 provides the first step. After telling us not to conform to the pattern of this world but instead be transformed by the renewing of our minds, Paul wrote, "*Then* you will be able to test and approve what God's will is—his good, pleasing and perfect will" (emphasis added).

Until I'm thus transformed, I won't even know what God's will is. If I allow myself to be conformed to this age, I won't *approve* of God's will and may even advocate against it—don't we see this happening in many corners of the church today? It's as simple as that.

So I must continually give my mind over to God's superior thoughts. I must dismantle what isn't true and always double back when I forget and take the wrong exit—*again and again.*

# STANDING OVATIONS

I've been on the speaking circuit for nearly three decades, where I've received many standing ovations, along with just polite applause a lot of times as well. I've learned that when you finish with a prayer, you pretty much kill the chance of a standing ovation (unless the host comes back up and asks for a second round of applause), so I usually end with a prayer.

I've been at a few conferences with another speaker who consistently gets standing ovations. Since I've heard most of the headliners and feel like I can do a decent job of evaluating both content and delivery, the standing-ovation thing surprised me. So I watched how this person ended several presentations and noticed three things this speaker always did at the very end of a talk.*

Though I'm somewhat embarrassed to admit it, I did those three things at the end of my next engagement and made sure not to close with a prayer. Sure enough—*boom!* There was a standing ovation. It made me laugh.

Just to preserve my soul, I stopped doing this.

Lisa heard my reflections on this, so you won't find me doing these things at a future engagement because Lisa will know I'm doing them. I may receive the endorphin rush of the crowd's momentary acclaim, but it will come at the cost of Lisa's contempt. She'll think (rightly so), "Seriously, Gary?" I don't want the world's acclaim if it elicits my wife's disapproval.

Turn this to a spiritual angle: Will you seek a standing ovation

---

* Other speakers have asked me what these three things are. I've purposely buried them, and so I no longer share them. It's not my mission to publicly critique someone.

from the world in the face of a God who sees what you are doing and disapproves of your motives, actions, and performance? You may become very successful in currying the favor of the world, getting the attention, appreciation, and reputation you desire, but a standing ovation from the world that comes with the contempt of your God is too costly. It's a poor choice.

I want to come out of the world to live in Christ. I want to feel the fresh breeze and smell the pure fragrance of a life devoted to Christ and affirmed by Christ. This is your invitation to join me in dismantling the lies we've mindlessly absorbed and in exchanging them for the better life in Christ. This is the life you were reborn to live.

# 1

# DISMANTLING
# RESTLESSNESS

## *Learn the True Path to Peace*

*Now may the Lord of peace himself give you
peace at all times and in every way.*

2 Thessalonians 3:16

Our friends are asking me the question directed to many people my age: "So what's your number?" "Your number" is the amount you hope to save up before retirement (which I'm not sure I'll participate in anyway). So you do what you're supposed to do and put money away instead of spending it all, slowly climbing toward that number—and then a bad economic year happens in the country, and 30 to 40 percent of your number disappears.

Poof. It's gone.

A little advice: Don't *ever* add up what you could have purchased (the vacation, the new car, the addition on the house) with that money. You'll just torture yourself.

Some friends of ours had millions saved up. It's a long story, but they're now paying rent (they had to sell their home), and it's a monthly struggle. The wife told me that Psalm 23:1 builds her up when money collectors tear her down: "The LORD is my shepherd, I lack nothing." Lacking nothing won't happen because they're going to hit their number. It won't happen because she and her husband are clever businesspeople who can earn it all back again. It won't happen because they have a huge inheritance coming (they don't). They'll lack nothing because God is their Shepherd, and that's a truth that will never change.

Peace is a person. It's not possessions, health, or acclaim. It's putting your security in a person and recognizing that if you have him, you already have enough. Even if you lose it all, even if nobody notices you, even if the world around you collapses, you already have everything you need.

Peace is so much better than money, acclaim, or even favor with your loved ones.

After that really bad investment year a while back, I exchanged anxiety for peace. I already have something much better than my "number." I have peace in God.

God desires all his children to experience deep, soul-refreshing peace. He grieves that we allow anxiety to pollute our thoughts and ruin our days. Has anxiety ever served you? Even once? Psalm 23:1 isn't just about money; it's about relationships, fulfillment, your loved ones. It's about everything you need: "I lack *nothing*."

When God's peace washes over me and I know I don't need anyone else's approval; I don't need my loved ones to make the decisions I want them to make to follow God; I don't need to perform to secure a happy eternity; I don't need a book to sell a certain number of cop-ies—I don't need anything that I don't *already have*—it's like losing fifty spiritual pounds. It's amazing!

My life was upended in a marvelous way when I learned that peace is relational, not situational. *Peace is a person.* When I could finally say, "Everything is well; all is okay; I have everything I will ever need at this very moment," I was able to stop striving, worrying, clawing, and fretting *right now.*

## A SUPERNATURAL SENSATION

Personal peace is among the highest spiritual experiences anyone can know. It is glorious, even supernatural. It is, I believe, one of the best things about being a Christian.

For our purposes, we can define personal peace as well-being in the widest sense of the word.* It means relative freedom (knowing there is no perfection in this world) from mental disturbance, anxiety, or lingering fear, no longer battling the feeling that the other shoe is about to drop, even when things are going well. Peace is a feeling, but it's more than a feeling. I describe it as a supernatural calm that all will be okay, even if everything around us is swirling in chaos. We're settled and at rest because we realize that our lives are in God's hands.

The fact that so few Christians experience this kind of peace, or even just a shadow of it, is one of the biggest omissions in Christian teaching today. I wonder if Jesus would say to the church today what he said to Jerusalem two thousand years ago: "If you, even you, had

---

* Peace is also biblically represented as reconciliation between Jew and Gentile (see Ephesians 2). There is significant implication for overcoming prejudice and racism in this biblical concept, but that would require a chapter on its own.

only known on this day what would bring you peace—but now it is hidden from your eyes" (Luke 19:42).

Not learning how to experience peace impacts our quality of life and greatly hinders evangelism. We spend so much time talking about salvation, but many people aren't interested in salvation because they can't see it and therefore don't believe in it. It's like somebody trying to sell you a "Best Of" album from a musician whose music you can't stand. Even if it is their very best, you still don't want it.

But everybody wants peace; they just don't know how to get it, because they must first dismantle the world's notion of where peace comes from.

Too many people think peace is dependent on the following:

- a pain-free life
- a problem-free life
- a stash of cash stored away to last a few decades
- a spouse who loves you and always treats you well
- children who appreciate you (and all of whom follow God)
- parents who are proud of you
- a vocation or financial portfolio that makes others respect you
- people in your life who don't hate you or oppose you
- people in your life who don't make you feel guilty or challenge your behavior
- the person or political party you favor currently holds office

False peace is thinking that if you can somehow make all these things come true, then you'll have peace. So that's what you focus on—striving to make these things happen. Withhold even one of these, and the result is agonizing anxiety. Withhold a couple, and you may even collapse into despair.

These things will never all be true at once, and even if none of them are true, you can still know peace. If you think you need to fix everything in your life to finally have peace, you'll never have peace. The peace God offers is entirely separate from our circumstances and is based solely on our relationship with him. Jonathan Hefner puts it this way: "It may not be well with my circumstances, but it is well with my soul."*

## A MOST BEAUTIFUL DESIRE

> You will keep in perfect peace
> those whose minds are steadfast,
> because they trust in you. (Isaiah 26:3–4)

When Jesus' followers learn the path to peace, they demonstrate to those with blinded eyes or hardened hearts that Jesus has arrived and therefore everything—*everything*—is different for those who place their trust in him.

Steve and Rebecca, two dear friends of mine, always appreciated Ruby's customer service as a cashier at a local grocery store because Ruby personified joy and peace—welcoming each shopper and openly sharing about God.

During the COVID-19 chaos, Steve and Rebecca went through Ruby's checkout line and asked how she was doing.

"Oh, I'm okay, considering," she said.

"Considering what?" Steve asked.

"My son is in the hospital on a ventilator with the coronavirus.

---

* Jonathan Hefner is a Substack reader of mine who read an early version of this manuscript.

He has an autoimmune disease, so the doctors are very worried about him. His prognosis isn't good. And of course, I can't visit him. Then yesterday, my doctor informed me that I have cancer."*

Ruby continued to ring up their groceries after sharing news that would have left most people shattered.

"We'll be sure to pray for you and your son," they said.

Ruby replied, "Thank you. I believe God has a purpose for all of this, and he has everything under control. You two have a blessed day."

The *Journal of the American Medical Association* reported that during the early days of COVID-19, "Mortality rates for those who received mechanical ventilation in the 18- to-65 and older-than-65 age groups were 76.4% and 97.2%, respectively."[1]

Three-quarters of young people and nearly all the elderly who went on ventilators never got off them. Ventilators were a last-ditch effort that failed far more often than it succeeded. On top of that, Ruby had just been diagnosed with cancer. Either one of these threats on their own would make most people unsettled. Balancing both at the same time would overwhelm most.

Yet Ruby lived with an assurance that God had a purpose for all this, and even more importantly, that God had everything under control. Because she knew God was in control, Ruby wasn't letting her emotions be controlled by her circumstances. So rather than panic and make her life the focus, she actually blessed Steve and Rebecca: "You two have a blessed day."

My friends were amazed to see such a deep peace during such a traumatic season. Ruby's personal life was harrowing, but she had peace.

Rebecca grew a little concerned when she didn't see Ruby on her next couple of visits to the grocery store, so she was overjoyed when

---

* Rebecca Wilke tells this story in her book *I Choose Hope* (SonKist Ministries, 2023).

she saw her on another trip and made sure to get in Ruby's line. She asked how Ruby's son was doing. Ruby said he had survived and was off the ventilator, though still in rehab. She also said her doctor had recommended a plan for her cancer treatment that had given her some assurance. Ruby then pointed to the T-shirt she was wearing under her employee vest, which touted a line from the *Chosen* series. It's from a scene in which Jesus admonished Peter, "Get used to different."

"I'm doing just that," Ruby exclaimed, her eyes (as Rebecca explains in her book) "sparkling with delight above the top of her mask."

"I'm getting used to different."

Are you anxious? Are you tired of always dreading the worst possible outcome? Do you lack a calm assurance that everything will be okay?

How about "getting used to different"?

## GOD'S PLAN FROM THE START

The coming of peace, the demonstrating of peace, and the embodying of peace in community have been God's plan from the very start. Isaiah foretold that the Messiah would be called the "Prince of Peace" (Isaiah 9:6). As God unfolded his plan of redemption, he promised that it would be marked by peace: "On David and his descendants, his house and his throne, may there be the LORD's peace forever" (1 Kings 2:33). A central prophetic message from Isaiah was, "'Peace, peace, to those far and near,' says the LORD" (Isaiah 57:19).

The psalmist declared, "The LORD blesses his people with peace" (Psalm 29:11). Peace is so central to who God is that he declares that his commitment to his people will be a "covenant of peace . . . an everlasting covenant" (Ezekiel 37:26). If you experience true peace for an hour, you feel immensely blessed. If you have an unbroken year of peace, you experience heaven on earth. But God promises a peace that is *everlasting*. There will never be a day—indeed, there will never be an *hour*—in which you have to give way to anxiety and fear-based foreboding. You have been set free from all that forever, from this day forward! That's what we have when *shalom*, God's favor, rests on us— his eternal smile and affirmation (which the New Testament tells us comes through Jesus). And this peace cannot be lost and will never end.

The Old Testament world was violent, wicked, disappointing, heartbreaking, and chaotic. Yet throughout the centuries, God promised his people, "Hang on. Peace is coming!"

God is true to his word. *When Jesus comes, peace comes.* The New Testament proclaims that peace is part of the new covenant. The heavenly host proclaimed to the shepherds that peace comes with the Messiah: "Glory to God in the highest heaven, and on earth peace to those on whom his favor rests" (Luke 2:14).

The early disciples emphasized peace in their preaching: "You know the message God sent to the people of Israel, announcing the good news of peace through Jesus Christ, who is Lord of all" (Acts 10:36).

The early church preached peace. Nineteen of the twenty-one letters in the New Testament begin or end with an exhortation to, or blessing based on, peace. The New Testament writers lived with the thought of peace on the tips of their tongues, giving it as an encouraging opening word or offering it as a comforting closing word to those they loved.

We know Jesus, they said, so we know peace.

*When we proclaim peace, we proclaim the arrival of God's kingdom, Jesus' reign, and the Holy Spirit's comfort.*

It is so crucial for you to experience this peace. Peace is a proclamation. Peace is a policy. Peace within and among God's children reveals the Prince of Peace. Our feet become "beautiful" when they walk to proclaim peace (Isaiah 52:7).

You want more? When we have this peace, we can go to sleep utterly defenseless and still not be anxious because the source of our peace is not asleep: "In peace I will lie down and sleep, for you alone, Lord, make me dwell in safety" (Psalm 4:8), and "He who watches over [you] will neither slumber nor sleep" (121:4). Whenever I have a momentary lapse and anxiety begins to build, I repeat the opening line of Psalm 23, "The Lord is my shepherd" and remind myself, *He will take care of me.*

Peace is a defining quality of life in Christ. And if we want to bear witness to the world of the coming of Christ, we must display a supernatural peace.

The thing is, peace doesn't come from where this age tells us it comes from—desperately trying to fix our lives so that nothing will bother us. We must unlearn that. We need to learn the peace that says, "Even if *it's* not okay, *I* will be okay."*

Peace comes from this:

> The Lord bless you
> and keep you;
> the Lord make his face shine on you
> and be gracious to you;
> the Lord turn his face toward you
> and give you peace. (Numbers 6:24–26)

Peace isn't found in prosperity, a pain-free existence, or people's approval; peace is found when God turns his face toward us and we fix

---

* I've heard others say this, but I first came across it in Kay Warren's book *Choose Joy* (Revell, 2012), 155.

our thoughts on him. Jesus tells us, "Peace I leave with you; my peace I give you" (John 14:27). Jesus can give us peace because, through his death, he has removed the wrath of God from our shoulders and ushered us into God's favor (Romans 5:9–11). This is the most important truth, the defining fact, of our lives. And since it's rooted in a finished work and a completed declaration, we live calmly out of the truth that what matters most is completed and locked down. If everything else is going wrong, the fact that things are right with God supersedes all else.

What if everything you own was wrenched out of your arms? What if your closest friends deserted you? What if there was a sentence of death hanging over you? What if Satan was making you his primary target for the moment?

Could you know peace even then? Yes, you could. I've just described Jesus, who personifies peace.

Christian peace isn't a problem-free life; it's a passionate life. Peace isn't found in changing our circumstances; it's found in changing our focus—*from* circumstances *to* a person.

It is rooted in relationship.

That's fine in theory, but how do we get there? How do we unlearn what we *think* leads to peace and learn to value what really does bring peace? When the psalmist urges us to "*seek* peace and *pursue* it" (Psalm 34:14, emphasis added), he is assuming that peace can be elusive. We don't have to seek and pursue something that's already in our possession.

As we look at those around us and feel the swirling tornado of anxiety in our own souls, we know that while peace is what we are born to crave, for most of us it is an occasional visitor rather than a constant companion.

How do we *seek* peace? How do we *pursue* it?

# THE PATH TO PEACE

If you want to experience rest, personal peace, and the blessed settled conviction that all will be well, even if all aspects of your life seem to be spinning out of control, I invite you to review nineteenth-century writer Henry Drummond's magisterial essay *Pax Vobiscum* (*Peace Be with You*). Drummond lays out Christ's recipe for rest and personal peace in a practical and insightful step-by-step journey.

For Drummond, gaining peace is like baking a cake—ingredients must be mixed and put through a certain process. When we do that, a cake (peace) results.

## 1. Remove Restlessness

Makes sense, right? To have rest and peace, we must first remove restlessness. There's a spiritual condition that results in restlessness—and a spiritual condition that results in restfulness. Henry Drummond reminded us, "Restlessness has a cause,"[2] and so to enjoy true and lasting peace, we must attack the cause.

What makes us restless? The constant and desperate demand to fix our circumstances. You won't find restfulness and peace while pursuing things that naturally breed anxiety.

Vihaan* was a young, successful orthopedic surgeon who taught internationally when he received notice that he was being sued for malpractice. He was served just minutes before going into the operating room to perform another surgery. Would this end his career? It would at least taint it, right? Vihaan fought back mentally, telling himself, *I need to think about what I'm doing right now; this patient deserves my full attention.*

Vihaan battled his initial concerns to successfully complete the

---

* Not his real name.

surgery, but the lawsuit unleashed a two-year journey of lost sleep, anxiety, anger, and sometimes a distracting sense of dis-ease.

This particular patient had fallen and come into Vihaan's operating room with a piece of broken elbow sticking out of his skin. Vihaan was able to save the elbow but couldn't avoid nerve damage, and the patient sued Vihaan for malpractice. He had a savvy lawyer who knew to request a relatively low amount—$50,000. The hospital's insurer estimated it would cost three to four times that amount to litigate, and so they did what they often do—namely, settle outside of court. But that, of course, left a mark on the surgeon's record.

I talked to Vihaan a few years after the suit and asked him how much it had impacted his career on a scale of one to ten.

"Zero," he said. He's still practicing, still teaching.

It's part of the trade. Very few, if any, surgeons will go through an entire career without being sued, and many hospitals will settle when the requested payoff is cheaper than litigation would be.

So we talked about how the *two years* of anxiety, sleepless nights, and fretful worries ended up being about . . . nothing. If Vihaan could talk to his younger self, he'd say the worries, fears, and concerns about his reputation and livelihood were all for naught. They accomplished nothing, but they hurt Vihaan a lot. They took his focus away from his family, his marriage, and sometimes his job.

For two years!

Vihaan knew he had done well in the surgery, but his restlessness was rooted in the loss of reputation, a perceived risk to his career, and potential embarrassment. If you remove those concerns, there would have been nothing—absolutely nothing—for Vihaan to fret about, and he would have had two more years of peace to look back on.

If your peace rests on the condition that no one will sue you, treat you unfairly, lie about you, or attack you, you'll never have peace.

What is your anxiety giving you?

Nothing.

What does it cost you?

Plenty.

If you want peace, get rid of peace's enemies—acclaim, financial security, human affirmation, a problem-free life, your choice for a political office, physical comfort and well-being, emotional intensity in relationships, personal attractiveness (and forever looking younger than you are), success in your vocation, and pride in yourself and your family. Many of these are natural wants; they're not in and of themselves evil. Yet they can sabotage the enormous blessing of personal peace whenever you begin thinking, *When I finally achieve them, I will have peace.*

That's a lie. And desperately trying to make them all come true is the very thing keeping you from peace.

## 2. Pursue Jesus: "Come to Me . . . and I Will Give You Rest" (Matthew 11:28)

Rest is found in *relationship*. Isaiah promises that God "will keep in perfect peace those whose minds are steadfast, because they trust in [him]" (Isaiah 26:3).

As I said before, peace isn't found in changing your circumstances; it's found in changing your focus.

Imagine being in the middle of a hurricane. Your house has disintegrated. Furniture is flying all around you. You hear screams. You don't know when the storm will end. Can you feel the fear and vulnerability that flood your soul?

Now imagine Jesus entering the scene. He walks toward you and takes your face in his hands, looking into your eyes and offering assurance. Maybe you picture yourself climbing into his lap. I like to imagine a ten-foot-tall Jesus, who wraps his strong arms around me and tells me he's never letting go. He stands behind me like an immovable cliff, enfolding me in his arms.

With Jesus in the picture, how could we *not* have peace? His presence overcomes and overwhelms this earth's seeming chaos. Because we're experiencing this devastation and destruction *with him*, we still have peace because he is more significant than the storm. In fact, with his arms around me, I'm going to open my eyes and watch the show!

Unlearn the natural bent of defining your well-being by *what* is happening to you. Learn to define it by *who* is walking with you. Meditate on how much you have when you have Christ. John Calvin reminds us, "God as our Maker supports us by his power, governs us by his providence, nourishes us by his goodness, and attends us with all sorts of blessings."[3] God isn't going anywhere. God doesn't get tired. God won't stop supporting us, governing us, nourishing us, and attending to us. Focusing on those truths, how can we *not* experience peace?

## 3. Peace Is Acquired via a Process

Jesus said, "Learn from me . . . and you will find rest for your souls" (Matthew 11:29). We must *learn* to spiritually rest. We must *learn* how to "cook" personal peace in our "spiritual oven."*

Jesus shares two key ingredients that produce peace and lead to rest—his *gentleness* and *humility*. We must learn to value who Jesus is

---

* For those who enjoy word studies, I should mention that the word translated "peace" in John 14:27 is *eirene*, used in the LXX to translate the Hebrew word for *shalom*. Here in Matthew 11:29, the word for rest is *anapauo*, but the concepts of peace and rest are intimately connected. We can *anapauo* (rest) when we have *eirene* (peace). *Eirene* leads to *anapauo*. So though the words aren't identical, it's fair for Drummond to discuss them as if they are two sides of the same coin, because linguistically they are. When you want rest, you're seeking peace. When you find peace, you find rest.

and what Jesus did, for he is the one in whom we find peace. Here's Jesus' self-portrait: "Take my yoke upon you and learn from me, for I am *gentle* and *humble* in heart, and you will find rest for your souls" (Matthew 11:29, emphasis added).

People who lack gentleness and humility are weary and burdened. When they come to Jesus, who personifies gentleness and humility, they find rest, which is the mark of peace. It follows that if we will relationally connect to Jesus' character and then learn to practice this character (especially gentleness and humility), we gain peace, which leads to rest.

I forfeit peace and choose restlessness far too easily. It seems idiotic that I would ever *choose* restlessness, but it's the kind of thing I'm trying to unlearn. Lisa and I use a parking lot shuttle service at the Denver airport because it's cheap. But sometimes you get what you pay for. On a recent trip, they directed me down an aisle to park, and the only two spots I could find were too small because large cars had parked over the white lines. If we had managed to squeeze our car into the spaces, we wouldn't have been able to open our doors. Incompetent customer service frustrates me to no end but here's what I've learned: My frustration doesn't cure their incompetence. All it does is sabotage my peace and send my blood pressure soaring.

Must I fix the world's customer service problem in order to know peace? In the past, I had that attitude. I didn't yell at anyone—but I polluted my soul to no good purpose. Now I realize it's a losing game. I can even thank God for incompetent customer service because it gives me an opportunity to grow a valuable spiritual attitude in which I am notoriously weak. For me, this is something I must learn through repeated trial and error. I examine my response, see how silly it is and how vulnerable I've made myself, and then I think it through: *Did my response help things? Are my expectations realistic? Is this the way I want to be?*

Let's go back to these words: *Restlessness has a cause.* When we find our ambitions frustrated and our selfish hopes and wants dashed, when we feel slighted—either attacked or ignored—we lose our peace. We're agitated, maybe even unable to sleep. We feel the loss so deeply that our souls scream out in pain.

Gentleness and humility strike these assassins at their very core. Look at how clearly and simply the virtues of Jesus lead to rest and peace. As Henry Drummond put it, "Be lowly. The man who has no opinion of himself at all can never be hurt if others do not acknowledge him. Hence, be meek. He who is without expectation cannot fret if nothing comes to him."[4]

If I don't *expect* everyone to do everything I want them to (family members, work colleagues, church friends, other drivers on the road), I won't fret when they don't. I won't be harsh and lash out and blow my peace to smithereens.

If I don't *expect* to live in an Instagram house, not having one won't make me unhappy in whatever home I live in. If I don't *expect* the world to agree with me on everything, I won't be shattered when the candidate I vote for loses their election bid. If I don't *demand* that people notice, affirm, and thank me, I won't lose a single second fretting over the fact that they don't.

Arrogance makes us feel vulnerable and exposed and puts us at the mercy of a fallen, cruel world that loves to hate, lie, assault, and murder (socially and physically). If you must be recognized and praised to feel good about yourself, you will never have peace. Wrote Drummond, "There are people who go about the world looking out for slights, and they are necessarily miserable, for they find them at every turn—especially the imaginary ones."[5]

Have you ever met a person who scours WebMD to find out what's wrong with them? I'm the worst at this! Last week I noticed some internal bruising on my right palm. No doubt blood was coagulating beneath the surface because my heart was failing. Better hug my wife tonight and tell her I love her! But then I washed my hands, and my life-threatening ailment was cured. Apparently some moss had rubbed off the garbage barrel I had taken out to the curb.

If you look for something to be wrong with you, you'll find it every time. One study reported that 70 percent of medical students at least briefly suffered from "transient hypochondriasis," a persistent, unrealistic preoccupation with the possibility of having a serious disease.[6] Their intense focus and study of pathologies led 70 percent of them to misinterpret common and normal signs as evidence of life-threatening illnesses.

No longer looking for slights is like washing your hands to get rid of the moss instead of worrying all night until you visit the doctor in the morning, and she washes your hands.

Arrogant or insecure people look for spiritual slights: "What did *that* look mean?" "How come she didn't call?" "When is the last time I've heard thank you, after all I've done?" Your sense of well-being is in bondage to the way others treat you, notice you, or appreciate you. *If you look for slights, you'll find them.* And you'll chase peace out of your soul faster than a rocket leaves the earth.

Henry Drummond connected meekness (or gentleness) with a lack of expectations. When we have high demands for how others treat us and they don't meet them—maybe their thank-you wasn't enthusiastic enough, maybe they didn't come through for us as we thought they should, maybe they just disappointed us—we tend to act harshly (the opposite of gently). We become vicious when we think we've been treated viciously.

The brilliance of Drummond's insight is that the bad experience feared by the arrogant and unmeek person can in reality serve as a highway to rest and peace. But there's a catch. To know true peace, we must *value* peace. I'm going to repeat that to emphasize it. To know true peace we must *value* peace. Too many of us don't, or we don't value peace enough in comparison to the other things we value. We want peace *and* success. We want peace *and* affluence. We want peace *and* acclaim. We want peace *and* everything to go just the way we want it to. We want peace *and* a model family.

But the demand for these things works against our peace if peace isn't valued above them. That's like saying "I want to maintain a healthy weight *and* eat cake and ice cream after every meal. I want to keep my blood sugar down *and* drink six sodas a day. I want to have a healthy heart *and* live a sedentary life."

Remember, peace is based on believing that even if *it's* not okay, *I* will be okay.

Pursue peace and you might get success, affluence, acclaim, and a happy home or marriage. They're not inherently evil, by any means. But when you make them your primary pursuit and love, the pursuit itself will destroy your peace because you make yourself completely vulnerable to the causes of unrest.

Jesus' recipe for peace undercuts our former way of thought (that security is found in acclaim, comfort, affluence, and earthly affirmation). Drummond wrote, "The first effect of losing one's fortune is humiliation; and the effect of humiliation is to make one humble; and the effect of being humble is to produce Rest."[7] There is, then, a sense in which we value humiliation, not for the sake of humiliation, but for what it produces. So losing our physical fortune becomes a spiritual gain. If we value spiritual peace, we believe we will have come out on top.

If I ask you, "Do you want peace?" your first thought will be, *Of course!* If I tell you the path to peace is humiliation (so that you can get over your dependence on the opinion of others), you're likely to say, *No, thank you.* We are lying to ourselves when we say we value peace if we don't value what brings peace. *It is a lie to say we want to be spiritually healthy if we strive after the very things that make us spiritually unhealthy.*

Does anybody doubt that Jesus had peace? He personified peace. Sleeping in the midst of a raging storm on the lake, making his way to Jerusalem even as he knew what lay ahead, leaving his immature disciples to carry out the Great Commission in the power of the Holy Spirit—this Jesus is the very picture of peace.

Did Jesus have money? No. Did Jesus have many enemies? Yes. Did Jesus have people plotting to kill him? Absolutely. Did Jesus have a close friend betray him? Of course. Did Jesus' disciples remain by his side during his vicious trial? No. Not even *one!*

Let's see—no money, lots of enemies, fair-weather friends, an unfair trial, a corrupt government, torture, and a death sentence.

And yet *peace?*

Drummond wrote, "Christ's life outwardly was one of the most troubled lives that was ever lived: Tempest and tumult, tumult and tempest, the waves breaking over it all the time till the worn body was laid in the grave. But the inner life was a sea of glass. The great calm was always there."[8]

Peace is found in who you *are*, not in what you *have.*

Peace is found in *whose* you are, in the one whose hand you are holding.

Peace is found in what you *value.*

Do you want to receive rest for your soul? First, remove the causes of restlessness, the anxiety-producing pursuits valued by the world. Second, fall into the arms of Jesus. Make him the center of your affections and thoughts. Define yourself by who he is, what he is to you, and who he has made you to be. Third, learn the process of rest. Keep letting go of pride, ambition, and the lust for fame, physical attractiveness, and financial security that actively and viciously work against your peace. Peace will elude you if you seek those things. And finally, pursue gentleness and humility. Stop asking the world to celebrate you or serve you. Focus instead on celebrating and serving Christ. Recognize that every seemingly bad thing in your life can produce good spiritual fruit if that bad thing is viewed through the lenses of humility and gentleness. You don't have to control everything. Don't insist that those around you love you perfectly. Go easy on yourself and others. You don't have to live a life of warfare, either against your own conscience or people who oppose you.

Following these four steps can escort you to the portal of peace right at this very moment. You simply have to say (and mean it), "I want peace more than I want acclaim. I want to be with Jesus more than I want anything or anyone else." Then keep walking in that direction until you get deeper into that attitude and into an unshakable peace and spiritual rest.

Compared to possessing this peace, how important is money, which can evaporate with one bad day on Wall Street? How important is public acclaim, which can turn on you like the crowds turned on Jesus, celebrating his arrival into Jerusalem and hours later demanding his crucifixion? You can't put a price tag on peace. If you've tasted it, you won't ever want to go back to living without it.

Reject the things that assault peace. Dismantle what you've been pursuing; welcome what brings peace. When you do, you will find spiritual comfort, personal rest, relaxation, and security.

As a final word, remember that we don't follow Jesus to get peace; we follow Jesus because he is truly divine, our creator and our rightful king. He is beautiful, and his beauty compels us to love him. As we love him, we experience the peace that naturally results from putting our trust in a kind, capable, and powerful God. If our only motive in following Jesus is to get peace, we'll get neither him nor peace. Jesus is the be-all-and-end-all, not the means to the end.

If we want to fully honor God and his Word, we need to start preaching peace to the church. It is far more crucial than we may think.

# 2

# DISMANTLING THE NEED
# TO BE IN CONTROL

## *Learn the Way of the Wind*

*The wind blows wherever it pleases. You hear its sound,
but you cannot tell where it comes from or where it is
going. So it is with everyone born of the Spirit.*

JOHN 3:8

Are you bored because nothing seems to be happening in your life
beyond your everyday routine?

Has Christianity started to feel lame and all too predictable?

Sometimes we think that to prosper in Christ we must control
everything around us—our schedule, temptations, relationships,
desires. Some teachers define *maturity* as maintaining and increasing
control over our lives.

But what if God calls us to *relinquish* our control?

We need to learn the blessed truth of the way of the wind. When we become Christians, we give up control of our lives and live by the credo of Jesus: "I have come down from heaven not to do my will but to do the will of him who sent me" (John 6:38).

Paul made this clear: "He died for all, that those who live *should no longer live for themselves but for him who died for them* and was raised again" (2 Corinthians 5:15, emphasis added). We no longer own our hours. We no longer get to set our own agenda. We no longer control what happens or when, and we must learn to ride the unpredictable but exciting wave of spiritual adventure. The wonderful thing about life in Christ is that it's more like driving an Uber than working a mail route—you never know who you'll meet or where you'll go next.*

I've had to dismantle the desire to control my day and my manipulations to make things happen. That's the way of the world. Disneyland is the self-proclaimed "happiest place on earth," but company lawyers do their best to make sure there are "no surprises" (i.e., lawsuits). Every ride must function as designed. Lines need to move according to their scheduled times. Animals are fed on the clock. If you hop on the "It's a Small World" ride in 2025, it'll be the same as it was in 1975 (and the song will be haunting you until 2055). You'll know what's around every curve and on every wall, and what you'll be told as you exit the boat.

Jesus' teachings and life paint a portrait that more closely resembles a jungle than a theme park in that you never know what's around the next bend or who you're going to meet next. You might crave an

---

* I'm indebted to Brian Jones for this quote, whose take is slightly different: "Following Jesus is more like driving a taxicab than being a librarian—you never know who you'll meet or where you'll go next" (*Second Guessing God: Hanging On When You Can't See His Plan* [Standard, 2006], 31).

occasional *visit* to Disneyland, but you were reborn as a Christian to *live* in the jungle. And it's only in the jungle that abundant life can be found.

If you're bored with the Christian life because it seems too routine and placid, you're likely not living the Christian life as it was meant to be lived. Frank Laubach (1884–1970) had an hourly goal to live in the presence of God and had an adventurous life accordingly. He wrote, "The notion that religion is dull, stupid and sleepy is abhorrent to God, for He has created infinite variety and He loves to surprise us. If you are weary of some sleepy form of devotion, probably God is as weary of it as you are. Shake out of it, and approach Him in one of the countless fresh directions."[1]

R. Somerset Ward (1881–1962), a beloved spiritual director in the Church of England, spent time and energy guiding people into life in Christ. He warned that life in Christ doesn't always look like a hyperorganized life:

> It is very easy, when everything we see round us is organized and limited, to fall into the habit of thinking that the same is true of the life of the Spirit. . . .
>
> Our Lord, when He was called upon to describe the spiritual life, took, as an illustration, the one phenomenon in our daily environment which is least ordered and limited. "The wind bloweth where it listeth, and thou hearest the sound thereof, but canst not tell whence it cometh and whither it goeth: so is everyone that is born of the Spirit." Here was a revolt, with a vengeance, against the neat, pigeon-holed, precepts of the Pharisees and the idea of the spiritual life as a system.[2]

Did you catch the word *everyone*? Christianity revolts against personal control. Christianity is based on humility and surrender to whatever God brings our way. This is an exciting life, a freeing life, and a dependent life. It's the life we are reborn to live.

Even so, this kind of living terrifies most of us. The "rule upon rule" of the Pharisees can be comfortable, easily understood, managed, and demanded: Don't do this, don't do that, pray here, work then, don't work at that time, this is what you wear, this is what you don't wear, this is what and when you eat and how you prepare your food. Such religion provides a safe, ordered world that we control. Under such a system, once God has written the rules and laid them out for us in a book, he can step out of the way for all we care and let us take over. In fact, we'll add a few rules of our own just to make sure we don't get too close to breaking God's rules.

But this is a life of fear, not faith. Ward wrote, "We have grown too tame; we are losing the spirit of adventure in religion."[3]

When was the last time you took a risk for God? When was the last time you stopped trying to accomplish twelve things on your to-do list and asked God what *one* thing he wants you to focus on right now? How this can set us free! We can be overwhelmed by not getting done all that we think we're supposed to get done, but when we pray, "Lord, what one thing should I do next?" excitement and determination replace defeat and despair.

When was the last time you shook your head in wonder after God used you in an entirely unexpected way, leading you to think, *Only God could have pulled this off*?

That may be the last time you truly worshiped.

The staff at Cherry Hills Community Church in Highlands Ranch, Colorado, knows I diligently prepare my sermons. It's even a bit of a joke to some of them. I usually do a run-through in front of a dozen people a few days before Sunday for a final tweaking. But much of the ministry that gets me jazzed about being there happens before, after, and between services, for which it's impossible to prepare. People come over to talk to me or ask for prayer. One dear woman with some developmental disabilities often tells me about her walk with God and her most pressing concerns. When I prayed for her over a deep sadness in her life, she said, "Wow! That prayer went right through me. I could feel the warmth of Jesus surrounding my heart." Another man came up and reminded me of a prayer I had prayed for him nine months earlier. In all honesty, I had forgotten about it, but he said it changed his life (also, he didn't say a single word about the sermon!).

I can't prepare for these times of ministry, nor can I make them happen. This type of ministry reflects the ministry Jesus did far more than my sermon prep does. The Gospel accounts are a whirlwind of Jesus going from person to person in a seemingly spontaneous or even haphazard fashion. Not once do we see him preparing for the Sermon on the Mount (unless, of course, you count the long sessions in prayer).

After one of our services, Jing,* a dear woman from China and member at Cherry Hills, felt led to volunteer at our Trailhead Ministry, which provides a place in the worship center where people can go for prayer, counsel, or information about our church. That Sunday, we had a female visitor present who spoke Cantonese but very little English. Her visit "just happened" to be Jing's first week to volunteer at this ministry, and Jing is fluent in Cantonese. The visitor was stunned to have someone she could talk to. Cherry Hills couldn't have planned this or anticipated how to help a woman from a foreign country find a sympathetic ear in the Denver area. Jing's first week of volunteering was what many people affectionately call a "God thing."

Life in Christ invites individuals and churches to unlearn the need to control what happens and instead dive headfirst into spiritual

---

* Not her real name.

adventure. If we're bored, it's quite likely we have little adventure in our lives. Fighting to stay in control means we have replaced God's exciting adventures with our own.

Recharge your faith with William Carey's famous challenge: "Attempt great things for God, and expect great things from God."[4]

# SAILING

What's the point of having a sailboat if you keep it tethered to the dock and never take it out on the water? Sure, there may be a storm once you leave the harbor. You may run into high waves. You risk getting the boat beat up by hitting a submerged stump or losing your navigation system and having to find your way back on your own. Danger may await, since water is often unpredictable. But boats are built to sail, and Christians are born for spiritual adventure, as R. Somerset Ward reminded us:

> A religion which centred around the life of Jesus Christ could never cease to be a religion of discovery. The whole of His life and teaching is one mass of exploration and adventure, and in no point perhaps are our lives more unlike His than in this feature. Too often our real desire is to find a safe stopping-place where we can abide, rather than a base for further advance. Nevertheless, God has placed in us a certain restlessness, physical and spiritual, necessary alike to body and soul, which will not leave us content with stability. It is for us to stimulate and use this divine dissatisfaction.[5]

I can stay busy all on my own. My own agenda can fill my thoughts, hours, and squares on the calendar. But that kind of life—busy and always feeling like I'm lagging behind—is exhausting and frustrating rather than energizing and exhilarating. It makes me want to give up rather than step up.

Do you, like me, ever feel the restlessness that Ward labeled "divine dissatisfaction"? *Learn to use that feeling.* Consider it God's call to experience a new abundance of adventure. Perhaps you've been settling for much less and God is now waking you up to new possibilities. He has already given you some victories, but what if he wants to give you even more? He has already used you to spread his kingdom, but what if he wants to give you a larger role? He has already opened a new world to you, but what if he wants to lead you to a new universe?

Dismantle your obsession with control. Learn instead to be astonished by the new things God is calling you to, things you could never plan or execute on your own.

Imagine waking up tomorrow and asking God to send someone your way who has need of something only you can provide. Maybe it's a word of encouragement, a few dollars, a smile, an hour or two of hard labor. But every day *you're looking.* You're anticipating some great (or even relatively quiet but still meaningful) move of God. That's life in the spiritual jungle.

I'm grateful to God for times of public ministry, whether giving a talk or sermon, writing a blog post or book, or pastorally counseling someone. But there's just something different about spontaneous ministry—something I didn't and couldn't plan, where I see God move and I see myself as an outside observer as God does something special. Those kinds of quiet miracles (heaven breaking into earth) hit my soul in an entirely different sphere and further cement my confidence and faith in God.

These are precious moments in Christ because I'm convinced we *need* spontaneous adventures. For one, they tend to blow away our intellectual doubts. By now, I've concluded that if God isn't real, then I am certifiably insane because otherwise I'm having a running conversation and daily dependence on, well, nothing. When God proves and re-proves himself day after day after day, one disappointment isn't going to shake my faith.

Living an abundant life of spiritual adventure is what we're designed to do: "We are God's handiwork, created in Christ Jesus to do good works, which God prepared in advance for us to do" (Ephesians 2:10).

My least favorite summer jobs growing up were any jobs that had a lot of downtime. I'd rather be busy than bored. Watching the clock is literally wishing our lives away. It's spiritually debilitating.

When we live our lives watching the clock, just passing the time without purpose—perhaps having a daily quiet time, going to church, and occasionally volunteering at a big church event, but primarily just hoping for heaven—it's like a job where we're fixated on the clock. It may even begin to feel like a wasted life. Dismantle that life!

Learn a new life. No matter where you are—on vacation, driving to work, shopping, arriving at church, taking a walk around the block— remind yourself, "The wind blows wherever it pleases" (John 3:8).

## ADVENTURE INJECTIONS

R. Somerset Ward acknowledged that real life can at times feel like being in prison. We have jobs, responsibilities, and appointments. We have things we must do even when we don't want to do them. But adventure can still penetrate and enrich our lives when we live with abundant expectations: "We have to get up and come down to breakfast every day, but the state of mind and attitude towards life with which we do so is capable of infinite variation."[6]

Maybe you have a relatively mindless job that feels monotonous and unfulfilling. Or maybe you feel shackled to your bed by ill-health. What if you asked God to place people on your heart who need prayer at *that very moment*? There may be stirrings in your mind until suddenly you come alive and plead with God to give strength, wisdom, discernment, and protection as he leads. A certain intimacy can erupt when we secretly partner with God to complete his work in someone else's life.

Ward pictured "some poor sleepless mortal lying on a bed of sickness, supposed by those around to be helpless and powerless, and yet being the means whereby a life is changed and a miracle worked. . . . Scattered over this country and over the wide world there are to be found souls waiting for the connecting link of your prayers. Will you let them wait in vain? Will you let souls wait outside while you neglect to pray?"[7] See the adventure?

Let's say your job requires you to interview someone or you're just catching up with a friend over a cup of coffee. Ward offered this insight:

> If we approach the conversation with a settled conviction that it is part of the regular task to be got through as usual, we are losing a chance. Each conversation is a potential adventure, capable of momentous results. All through the day which seems so fixed and so ordinary, avenues are continually presented to us for a journey into a far country. At every cross road we pass there are miracles waiting round the corner. We can neither see nor use them unless we keep a living spirit of enterprise and expectation in our souls.[8]

What if it turned out you're not just delivering a package, picking up an Uber client, or having lunch with a coworker? What if God had mapped out this encounter to be something far more?

Fair warning: You will drive yourself crazy if you demand this kind of experience every hour of the day or perhaps even every day. The wind does blow *as it pleases*, but to never live with such expectations is just as foolish as always demanding them.

My desire to experience a deeper life in Christ means I want to be more spiritually adventurous, which means being more loving, more available, more helpful, and more servant-hearted. It also means giving up control so that God can take me wherever he chooses to take me.

A spiritually adventurous life requires risks, what R. Somerset Ward called intentional daily experiments: "If I limit my efforts to what I have always done, my charity will be what it has always been."[9] Let's say you've routinely given 5 percent or 10 percent of your income to charitable causes, but what if God presents you with an opportunity to be bolder in your giving? You've had success interacting with certain kinds of people in certain kinds of situations, but what if God wants to expand the borders of your ministry? You've gained victory over a particular area of darkness, but what if God wants to shine a light in a new corner of your life?

If we realized what we forfeit by refusing to embrace a spiritual adventure, we might gain the courage to take the next step. Ward's words haunt those who timidly refuse to live the abundant life in Christ: "We are like sleep walkers, wandering with shut eyes, through a world full of opportunity for our souls."[10]

Stay-at-home parents and two-job single parents, office drones, pastors of small churches, and government nonessential workers can live adventurous lives, propelled along by the winds of the Spirit that make every encounter pregnant with profound possibility. Hearing from God to encourage, support, strengthen, confront, and comfort at just the right time in just the right place ushers divine force into lives formerly buried under small thinking.

If you want to study the idea of spiritual adventure a bit further, I suggest you pick up a copy of *Hudson Taylor's Spiritual Secret*.[11] Some may think he took some of his risks too far (I don't see what's wrong with asking your boss for your rightful pay rather than simply praying about it), but he exemplified a life of spiritual adventure.

Frank Buchman, the founder of Moral Re-armament, was another notable historical figure whose life demonstrated a commitment to spontaneous spiritual adventure. While his ministry wasn't without controversies, his openness to being used by God in stunning, spontaneous ways can teach a transformative lesson to those for whom ministry is all about planning and control. I recommend you read Buchman's biography, *Frank Buchman: On the Tail of a Comet*, written by Garth Lean.[12] You might also enjoy Garth Lean's memoir of his own work with Moral Re-armament titled *Good God, It Works! An Experiment in Faith*.[13]

## WHERE ARE WE GOING?

In his book *Unoffendable*, Brant Hansen tells a story about a morning with his family in Houston. They buckled their kids in the car, went to a grocery store, dropped something off at a friend's house, and ran a few other errands. Along the way, Brant was pulled over for speeding.

After they got back on the road, his daughter asked him where they were going, and he said they were headed to the Houston rodeo to see horses. Then Brant thought about the entire morning through his daughter's eyes:

It dawned on me: How odd had this whole trip been, from her perspective? From the very outset, she'd just been sitting, buckled in, while we went here and there and everywhere. She'd just watched her mom run in and out, and a strange man approach the car with a funny hat and flashing lights, and we turned this way, and turned that way, and sped up and slowed down and sped up again.

And she had no idea where we were going. None. But she was cool with it.[14]

Brant compared his daughter's attitude to his own disposition (and that of most of us)—always wanting to know where we're going, what's next, what's the purpose. And yet here was his daughter, letting her parents drive her around, ultimately bringing her to a very special destination—the largest rodeo in the world.

What if God wants to provide the same lifelong experience for us? What if we never outgrew a child's humble acceptance of letting her Father drive her around? Can we relearn to be as trusting as Brant's daughter, giving up control of our lives and letting "Jesus take the wheel"?

It's the distinctive line between a life of mistrust, stress, exhaustion, anger, bitterness and ceaseless striving, and a life of contentment and rest. Not just for her but for all of us who know that, ultimately, we're not in control:

*She knew who was driving.*

She knew, and still knows, that the one who is driving . . . loves her.

And that makes all the difference.[15]

# 3

# DISMANTLING
# FAMILY FIRST

*Learn the Preeminence of Father God*

> *I am a foreigner to my own family,*
> *a stranger to my own mother's children;*
> *for zeal for your house consumes me,*
> *and the insults of those who insult you fall on me.*

PSALM 69:8–9

Nobody warned us what was coming. In fact, we were often promised the opposite. What we heard was that being good, pious Christians and hyperinvolved parents would create a good, pious family, all of whom would follow the Lord and raise grandchildren who would do the same. The implication is that if we are faithful in serving God, all our descendants will be as well.

I can't count the number of times thirty or forty years ago when someone would point to Congregationalist preacher Jonathan Edwards, whose faith and life produced many impressive descendants, including fourteen college presidents, more than a hundred ministers, another hundred college professors, and so on. I *wasn't* told that Jonathan Edwards owned slaves. And so the slavery issue for Edwards blew the "example" theory (be faithful and your progeny will be faithful) part to bits. Real life has a way of seriously challenging that promise.

It wasn't until I became an empty nester myself and had friends who are empty nesters that I began hearing other stories and perspectives. One earnest father with a broken heart told me, "Gary, I can't think of hardly any Christian parents with adult kids whose hearts haven't been seared by their children's lifestyle or their rejection of their faith."

When a woman working for a major national ministry shared with me her grief over the pain of a son's recent decision, I shared this father's quote to encourage her. She paused and said, "Actually, *none* of my three boys are following the Lord."

A counselor told me about the godliest couple he had ever known, the kind of people who bring the presence of Jesus into every room. They were beloved at their church. God used them to heal many marriages and offer counsel to many young people who sought them out. "Their faith was so genuine and powerful and inviting," the counselor told me, "it was amazing." Yet when the woman died, an entire year went by before her estranged son even knew it. He was *that* estranged. An entire church mourned his mother's passing, and yet for her son, his mother's funeral was just like any other day ending with *y*. His absence at the service was painful and shocking.

Learning the preeminence of "Father God"—who is our first, primary, and most important "family" relationship—leads to lives that are stable and secure because our acceptance in Christ is certain and cannot be lost. Putting our sense of well-being and happiness in the hands of fallen people—even people who share our bloodline—is precarious, risky, and hazardous to our peace. It's like fool's gold that sparkles from a distance, but when we see it up close, its lack of eternal value becomes clear. We must dismantle the desperation we feel for earthly families to fulfill us and learn instead how to be fulfilled in the spiritual family into which God adopts us.

Life in Christ will lift us up when loved ones let us down. God will draw us close when those we love the most push us away. The same psalmist who wrote, "I am a foreigner to my own family, a stranger to my own mother's children; for zeal for your house consumes me, and the insults of those who insult you fall on me" (69:8–9), found comfort in the God who is always there: "I pray to you, LORD, in the time of *your favor*; in *your great love*, O God, answer me with *your sure salvation.* . . . Answer me, LORD, out of the goodness of *your love*; in *your great mercy* turn to me" (vv. 13, 16, emphasis added). While admitting the pain of family estrangement, the psalmist bathes in God's glorious affirmation and love.

Life in Christ hinges on the notion that Jesus claims not just our *first* allegiance but our *entire* allegiance. Our commitment to our family is a subset of our commitment to God, not vice versa. We shouldn't try to use God to get the family we want ("we'll pay lip service to you, God, if you just keep us all happy and united"). Rather, we put our family on the altar, along with everything else, so we can be 100 percent surrendered to our Lord, Master, and King.

Jesus doesn't promise that faith will always bring families together. On the contrary, "Brother will betray brother to death, and a father his child; children will rebel against their parents and have them put to death. You will be hated by everyone because of me, but the one who stands firm to the end will be saved" (Matthew 10:21–22).

Some of us must learn that God—simply God—is good enough

for us, even if there is no family alongside us. It is a true blessing when we can have both God and close family relationships—heaven on earth! One of my happiest moments was sitting in a small church, glancing up during worship to see my then three teenage children worshiping God, two raising their hands in praise. Another incredibly happy moment for me was the summer all three were involved in missions opportunities. Not much can be more fulfilling than that. It is natural to want that. But what we are *promised* is God, and God alone; what we are *warned* about is putting family before God.

Job did not curse God when his children physically died, and we must not curse God if our children spiritually die. And we must never join them in their spiritual death by choosing them over God.

## THE PERILS OF EARTHLY FAMILIES FIRST

If we don't dismantle what we've been told (often in the church) about a certain kind of guaranteed family life, we may lose our greatest solace when family life falls apart.

Abusive parents have blinded many to the loveliness of a Father God who describes himself this way: "The LORD, the LORD, the compassionate and gracious God, slow to anger, abounding in love and faithfulness, maintaining love to thousands, and forgiving wickedness, rebellion and sin" (Exodus 34:6–7). People who had abusive parents are sometimes angry at God for not giving them better families. Rather than letting that anger turn into bitterness, how much better would it be to worship the God who offers them the perfect spiritual family.

God never promises us a perfect earthly family. The Old Testament revelation, in fact, begins with a string of grotesquely dysfunctional families. God promises us a perfect God to help us cope with imperfect families. If we think earthly families are of first importance, we will *turn on* a God who denied us a loving family rather than *turn to* a God who rescues us from the lack of the same.

The teaching that we should put family first has kept some women in abusive marriages they should have left long ago. Their bodies were damaged, their ministries quenched, and their souls diminished. The spiritual fruit they might have borne fell to the ground. Some in the church lectured them about their marital commitment while essentially ignoring their spiritual commitment to their Savior, and it broke God's heart. I am not excusing divorce that results from mere difficulties or disappointments. As the author of *Sacred Marriage* and numerous other books on marriage, I hope that's clear.* All I'm saying is that as vital as marriage is, it cannot even compare to our calling to a relationship with God.

If you think it sounds unbiblical to distinguish between staying true to a marriage or true to a divine calling, your argument isn't with me; it's with Jesus: "'Truly I tell you,'" Jesus said to them, 'no one who has left home or wife or brothers or sisters or parents or children for the sake of the kingdom of God will fail to receive many times as much in this age, and in the age to come eternal life'" (Luke 18:29–30). "For the sake of the kingdom of God" definitely does not mean for promoting our own happiness, overcoming our own disappointment, or getting out of a frustrating relationship and marrying someone new.

The teaching that we should put family first has led some parents to make significant moral compromises to try to keep their families together. Some have denied what they previously believed regarding the teachings of Christ and his apostles, even changing their own theology just to stay on good terms with their children and not lose access

---

* I unpack the distinction I'm implying here in several chapters of my book *When to Walk Away* (Zondervan, 2019).

to grandchildren. They have forsaken the commandments of God for the opinions of their children and thus betrayed not just their God but their children as well.* Please understand, I'm in no way suggesting we should reject our families; let's do all we can to keep loving them. I'm just warning—as Jesus does—that they may reject *us*.

Putting family first has kept some earnest believers who suffered broken marriages—or who were sinned against by a previous spouse and thus divorced—from fully serving God as empowered servants of the church. When their spouse left or betrayed them, some in the church did too. It is curious logic that disqualifies someone for official ministry because of something someone else does to them. I've met people who loved their former spouse heroically only to be forced to admit that the person they married was morally incapable of being a faithful or nonabusing spouse. They may have been guilty of making a poor marital choice (but then again, maybe they were simply fooled by a very clever con artist), but does falling in love and making a poor choice mean you can't be ordained to serve God once the consequences of that poor choice have grown to fruition?

Being unfaithful is one thing and does require careful analysis for future office; being a *victim* of unfaithfulness is an entirely different matter. It would be monstrous for courts to convict and sentence both the perpetrator and the victim of a crime. Yet historically some groups in the church have treated both participants of divorce this way when it came to establishing who is qualified for ministry.

Lastly, putting family first plays into Satan's hands, who will sometimes use our families to put an obstacle in our way toward serving God. Richard Baxter warns, "If [Satan] can, he will . . . stir up

---

* As a grandparent myself, I don't mean this to sound harsh. I understand the temptation to put family peace first. But however alluring the pull, we must hold to the truth and be faithful to God.

thy own father, or mother, or husband, or wife, or brother, or sister, or children, against thee, to persuade or persecute thee from Christ: therefore Christ tells us, that if we hate not all these, that is, cannot forsake them, and use them as men do hated things, when they would turn us from him, we cannot be his disciples."[1]

Luke's gospel contains a chilling phrase after Satan tried to bring Jesus' earthly ministry to an end and failed. So Satan then went after one of the closest companions of Jesus: "Satan entered Judas, called Iscariot, one of the Twelve" (Luke 22:3). While Judas wasn't an immediate family member of Jesus, you can make an argument that the Twelve had a closer relationship than that of many nuclear families. It's not far-fetched to think that if Satan can't get to us, he'll seek to influence someone close to us—including a family member. Spiritual warfare is real, and Satan engages in it with a malicious vengeance.

In no way am I suggesting we refuse to sacrificially serve and be devoted to our earthly families. If an ambitious pastor or missionary ignores their spouse and children "for the sake of the kingdom," the kingdom they are building is not the kingdom of God but may well be one driven by selfish ambition. Loving God would compel them to care for their family sacrificially and to love their spouse as Christ loves the church.

I once counseled a former pastor who had made his congregations his mistresses and ignored his wife in the process. The damage ran deep, and he has a lot of work ahead of him to rebuild his marriage before he can even consider returning to ministry. And when a woman merely gets bored with her husband and denies the vows she made to God because she thinks there must be someone more exciting out there, it's a *grievous* sin. I've seen strong men reduced to tears, and I believe it elicits tears from God. How can you see the person made in your image overcome with grief and not be angry with the one who unjustifiably causes that grief?

Remember this: When I say we shouldn't put family first, I'm not saying we should put family last or even third. It's a hard second in my list of priorities. But it's not even a close second if we listen carefully to Jesus' words.

Another reason to dismantle putting family first is so you can avoid the vulnerability and confusion you will feel when a parent, sibling, or child attempts to shame you. You may begin to think you're somehow disqualified before God, even after all that Jesus has done for you (and even knowing your qualification is in him, not in yourself), because you've failed in some way those you love the most.

God's love for you is based on what Christ has done for you; it is not dependent on you being the perfect child, parent, spouse, or sibling. Instead of experiencing the joy, security, and happiness that come from defining yourself as chosen, accepted, and affirmed by God, if you define yourself by family failures, you'll be covered in shame, almost completely devoid of delight, hollowed out of peace, and barren in your worship. You'll avoid God because you think you are unworthy of him. After all, that's what your family told you: "You call yourself a Christian? After what you did/said/didn't do to me?"

Maybe you did fail your family, but *it doesn't make you a failure to God.* We all fail in many ways (James 3:2). Of course, we wish we could be the best children, parents, siblings, and spouses, but life in Christ means we will never be defined by *any* of our failures. We're defined by God's forgiveness and his adoption of us as his children.

God's Word spiritually divorces us from depending on our family's favor to lead us to depend on *his* favor, and his favor *alone*: "Though my father and mother forsake me, the LORD will receive me" (Psalm 27:10).

## HOLY HATRED

Jesus continued a long line of biblical teaching that places faith over family. In Deuteronomy, we read these words:

> If your very own brother, or your son or daughter, or the wife you love, or your closest friend secretly entices you, saying, "Let us go and worship other gods" (gods that neither you nor your ancestors have known, gods of the peoples around you, whether near or far, from one end of the land to the other), do not yield to them or listen to them. Show them no pity. (13:6–8)

Jesus emphasized this ancient teaching and broadened it to include both mission and faith. "Large crowds were traveling with Jesus, and turning to them he said: 'If anyone comes to me and does not hate father and mother, wife and children, brothers and sisters—yes, even their own life—such a person cannot be my disciple. And whoever does not carry their cross and follow me cannot be my disciple'" (Luke 14:25–27).

The Greek word for *hate* here (*miseo*) is Semitic hyperbole. Jesus is not telling us to hate our family members as people think of hating enemies—a passionate desire to harm them. Admittedly, the Greek word *miseo* really does mean "hate," but remember that Jesus spoke Aramaic, not Greek. *Miseo* is what Luke chose to use to translate whatever Jesus actually said in Aramaic into the Greek language. Also keep in mind that when Jesus urges us to have the same *miseo* toward our own lives, he is also making it as clear as possible that he never means to do ourselves or our family intentional harm or even to bear them ill will. That's not the kind of hate Jesus is talking about.

And yet if we say *miseo* means "love them less than we love God," that isn't strong enough. There's a reason Luke chose this word. He didn't want to dampen the seriousness or the shock of what Jesus was saying. The act of dismantling cannot happen here with a soft or polite word. The new world and the transformed life Jesus invites us into require something bold, strong, and even shocking.

Thus *miseo*.

God's kingdom, his work, our relationship with him, and his favor must become so significant, so enthralling, and so essential that nothing else is even a consideration in comparison. Far from causing us to love our families less, putting God first enables us to truly love them faithfully and sacrificially. Nuance matters. Saying faith comes first doesn't mean family comes last or family isn't important. Putting faith first helps us love our families best.

Consider the life of Jesus, who as he completed his work on the cross—undeniably the most important work ever accomplished by anyone on earth—took time to make sure his mother would be taken care of after he died, charging John to care for her as his own mother (John 19:26–27).

Astonishingly, Jesus wasn't so busy doing God's work that he was blinded or calloused to family obligations. But even this work is modified in that, at least according to Protestants, Mary had other children who could have stepped up to take care of her after Jesus died. In fact, Protestants count two authors of New Testament books—James and Jude—as sons of Mary, though they don't appear to be believers at the time of the crucifixion.* In commending Mary's care to John, who wasn't a blood relative,† Jesus places faith over genetic loyalty. Jesus was more concerned that his mother be cared for by a man who followed him and believed in him than by young

---

* The Roman Catholic Church holds that these men were not Mary's children but rather cousins of Jesus. The Eastern Orthodox Church teaches that they were half-siblings through Joseph, who fathered them before he married Mary; thus Jesus was Mary's only child.

† Some traditions suggest that John's mother was Mary's sister, thus making John a cousin of Jesus. I don't want to take sides on an issue that the text itself does not definitively decide.

men who were obligated by blood commitment but who may not yet have been worshipers of Jesus.

Life in Christ leads us to love our families with the right perspectives and in God-honoring ways.

## A HIGHER CALLING

For centuries, a Jewish woman felt no higher calling than to become the mother of the Messiah, yet look at how Jesus spoke of his own mother: "As Jesus was saying these things, a woman in the crowd called out, 'Blessed is the mother who gave you birth and nursed you.' He replied, 'Blessed rather are those who hear the word of God and obey it'" (Luke 11:27–28).

*Birthing and nursing don't matter as much as studying God's Word and obeying it.* Mary is revered by the historic church first and foremost for being Jesus' mother; yet Jesus said that true blessing comes from spiritually following the commands of God more than by physically giving birth to Jesus. Any woman who becomes an obedient servant is more than a mother; she is a disciple of God, which is valued even above motherhood.

Again, this is not to say mothering isn't important and shouldn't be celebrated. Mothering does matter. It is crucial and should be celebrated enthusiastically. In a culture that sometimes diminishes the worth of mothering, it makes sense to elevate this call. But as Christians we still hold to the truth that as valuable as motherhood is, it's not a woman's *first* call in life. It doesn't define a woman or determine her final worth.

Nor does fathering define a man. In the past, I taught that the most impactful thing a man can do is raise children who will serve God and raise their children to serve God. I still see this as a high ideal. One of the best, most strategic things we can do for the kingdom of God is raise children who will worship and serve God as well. But I was wrong to define a man by his child-rearing abilities. Jesus and Paul had a transformative impact on the kingdom of God without raising any children. And who was Moses's first child?

You don't remember?

I'll give you a hint: It starts with a *G*.

Still don't know?

Okay, it ends with *om*.

Still drawing a blank?

Fine, it was Gershom. The *only* thing we know about him is his name. But can anyone say that conceiving and raising Gershom was the defining characteristic of Moses's life?

Did Peter have sons and daughters? What about John or Andrew? And if they did have children, what did these children do? What do we know about them?

Kingdom-first living celebrates the family and urges us to be thoughtful, intentional, and even sacrificial parents, but it no longer defines us by our families in the way the Old Testament did with respect to Abraham, Isaac, Jacob, and so on.

Jesus clearly elevates kingdom living over blood fealty in the way he treated his blood relatives, including his mother.

> While Jesus was still talking to the crowd, his mother and brothers stood outside, wanting to speak to him. Someone told him, "Your mother and brothers are standing outside, wanting to speak to you."
>
> He replied to him, "Who is my mother, and who are my brothers?" Pointing to his disciples, he said, "Here are my mother and my brothers. For whoever does the will of my Father in heaven is my brother and sister and mother." (Matthew 12:46–50)

We are never told whether Jesus ever went out to speak to them.

Matthew didn't think it was important for us to know. I suspect Jesus did, but Matthew wants us to learn from this account that kingdom work and service are more important than family loyalty. There is no other way to understand this passage.

This is shocking to modern Christian sensibilities. But it wasn't so shocking to prior generations of believers. Thomas Brooks recounts a story from the mid-sixteenth century:

> In the time of the Marian persecution there was a gracious woman, who being convened before bloody Bonner, then bishop of London, upon the trial of her religion, he threatened her that he would take away her husband from her. Saith she, Christ is my husband. I will take away your child. Christ, saith she, is better to me than ten sons. I will strip you, says he, of all thy outward comforts. Yea—but Christ is mine, saith she, and you cannot strip me of him. Oh! the assurance that Christ was hers bore up her heart, and quieted her spirit under all.[2]

Putting family first would have made this faithful woman so vulnerable that she may have been tempted to renounce Christ. Putting God first gave her such a staunch resolution that there was nothing—literally nothing—her persecutors could threaten her with that could make her renounce her first love.

## SPLITTING FAMILIES

Simply quoting Jesus' words about our families of origin leads me to astonishment that we ever thought family should come first. The Bible tells of a man who wanted to follow Jesus but asked for some time to take care of a weighty matter: "'Lord, first let me go and bury my father.' But Jesus told him, 'Follow me, and let the dead bury their own dead'" (Matthew 8:21–22).

Commentators differ on whether this man's father was actually dead or simply aged, which would have meant that his desire wasn't to oversee the burial, but perhaps he was asking to wait a few years to start following Jesus (when, in fact, Jesus would already have gone to the cross). The man may have been asking, "Let me stay at home and take care of my parents, and after they die, I'll follow you."

Jesus rejected that line of thinking. Elsewhere in Scripture (1 Timothy 5:8), Paul commanded us to take care of our elderly parents, so this may have been a historic anomaly. After all, the time to follow Jesus while he was in the flesh was quickly passing. Or it may have been about a lack of enthusiasm on the man's part. And yet the invitation to follow Jesus is so glorious that we should look for a reason to make sure we respond without further delay. No matter how we interpret this passage in Matthew, Jesus clearly claims preeminence over earthly cares and concerns.

I grew up learning in church that Jesus is the uniter of families. I still believe this is true when we are joined in faith, belief, and worship. But Jesus also taught that faith in him will divide some families. Because allegiance to him is so absolute, those who reject Jesus will inevitably reject his disciples: "Brother will betray brother to death, and a father his child; children will rebel against their parents and have them put to death" (Matthew 10:21).

If we look down on Christian parents whose children have forsaken them, we call Jesus a liar. Jesus is telling us that children will betray their parents because their parents are faithful, not because they were neglectful, which isn't to deny that some children reject their parents' faith because of hypocrisy or abuse, even though the parents claimed to be followers of Jesus.

Jesus adds in even stronger language:

"Do not suppose that I have come to bring peace to the earth. I did not come to bring peace, but a sword. For I have come to turn

> "'a man against his father,
>> a daughter against her mother,
> a daughter-in-law against her mother-in-law—
>> a man's enemies will be the members of his own
>>> household.'

"Anyone who loves their father or mother more than me is not worthy of me; anyone who loves their son or daughter more than me is not worthy of me. Whoever does not take up their cross and follow me is not worthy of me. Whoever finds their life will lose it, and whoever loses their life for my sake will find it." (Matthew 10:34–39)

Far from faulting his followers when faith divides a family, Jesus tells his disciples they will be rewarded for it: "Everyone who has left houses or brothers or sisters or father or mother or wife or children or fields for my sake will receive a hundred times as much and will inherit eternal life" (Matthew 19:29).

The apostle Paul, who urged husbands to love with a heroic, martyr-like devotion to their wives (Ephesians 5:25; Colossians 3:19), also wrote, "From now on those who have wives should live as if they do not" (1 Corinthians 7:29). Paul wasn't being contradictory here. His point in 1 Corinthians 7 is that our faith takes such precedence in focus and importance that marriage is in reality a secondary issue. But secondary doesn't mean unimportant. Those who are married should be *devoted* spouses. We must not forget, however, that our first devotion, far and away, is the worship and work of Christ. Paul wrote, "I am saying this for your own good, not to restrict you, but that you may live in a right way in undivided devotion to the Lord" (v. 35).

I've devoted most of my adult life to trying to strengthen Christian marriages and families. In no way do I want to reject the sacrificial service we are called to or the sheer joy we experience in loving our families. If our grandchildren knew how often Lisa and I talk about them, plan to do special things for them, and even considered their welfare when buying a house, they would be amazed. When our children finish a phone conversation with "I love you guys," they have no idea how that one line can emotionally feed me *for days*. When my wife's picture pops up on my phone wallpaper, my heart can melt like it did when I was an infatuated college student. I continue to pour myself out in prayer and service to my family and will continue to do so *because* of my faith, not in spite of it.

But I can't love my family well if I don't love God, not just first, but overwhelmingly. What God wants for them is more important than what I want for them. Their relationship with God matters more than their relationship with me. I should be more concerned about their standing with God than I am about their view of or standing with me. If they start to waver in their faith in God and feel convicted by him, they will naturally feel uncomfortable around me. I hope it will never be because I'm acting like a pompous, self-righteous jerk who is a stranger to grace. Yet since so many people rejected Jesus in his day, parents are foolish to think that being like Jesus will mean their children will never reject them. Being like Jesus may be the catalyst for your children (or parents or spouse) to reject you.

Here's what I've become convinced of with regard to family life: The only thing that matters is God's favor and anointing. The question I ask is this: Am I trying to please God or my family members? Because devotion to God is the linchpin of my life, God may test my commitment. Family life may call me to make decisions that some in the church may question. My decision must be based on God's favor and God's anointing. The opinion of others shouldn't move me one millimeter if I'm doing what I'm doing out of obedience to God. On the other hand, my family may question and judge me for what I don't do, but that also shouldn't move me one millimeter.

I am to cooperate with God to love my family according to God's definition of what love means at that moment. If I am sincerely seeking his will, I believe he will be pleased with me, even if, perhaps, I misunderstand his will, as long as he knows I am sold out to him and his favor—that everything I do and say and decide is to honor him, please him, and worship him as my Savior and Lord. He deserves no less.

I long for my family's love, but I am first and foremost *dependent* on God's love. I enjoy my family's attention, but I am a stranded man in the middle of the desert with no hat, shirt, or water without God's attention.

Life in Christ is rooted in a passionate adherence, adoration, and dependence on the most beautiful, wonderful, powerful, and glorious Being there is. That's the first lesson we must learn. God's love defines us, sustains us, encourages us, uplifts us, and strengthens us. There is no more solid foundation known to humankind through which you can understand yourself. Therefore, we must let go of the alluring but false understanding that we are defined by our family of origin or our immediate family. Because the promise of family life can be so good and so enthralling, we must consciously and intentionally unlearn the temptation to view our family as our defining reality. Just as Abraham put his son Isaac on the physical altar, we must put our families on the spiritual altar, willingly relinquishing them at God's command and then hopefully receiving them back as God's gift. But in the end, they are God's gift to take away or provide. It all comes back to him.

# 4

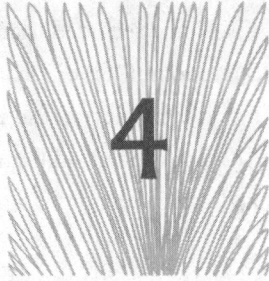

# DISMANTLING ISOLATION

*Become Relational Instead of Isolationist*

*I long to see you so that I may impart to you some
spiritual gift to make you strong—that is, that you and
I may be mutually encouraged by each other's faith.*

ROMANS 1:11–12

My parents used to live just a couple of miles from a Starbucks in Sumner, Washington. It became my preferred place to work early in the morning when I'd visit them. Months would go by between visits. But one time I showed up and was disappointed to see that the store had rearranged the layout, thus obliterating my usual writing spot. I used to sit at a small table in a far corner away from the door, conveniently located next to an electrical outlet where I could plug in my laptop and pretend I was on a secluded island. I could be invisible there and work without distraction. Since I had traveled from Texas, my body was functioning on Central time, so it wasn't unusual to be their first patron when they opened at 4:00 a.m. (6:00 a.m. Central time). I liked being tucked away with my laptop, my thoughts being my only companions.

My new perch was on the other side of the restaurant and was far more visible. One day, I saw a man, who looked to be in his mid-eighties, come in. He did the exact opposite of what I always do. He rearranged a chair, turning it around to face the door and the ordering line. He then moved a small table on which he placed his coffee. He remained three steps from the door and four steps from the counter so no one could go in or out without seeing him and greeting him. He knows the regulars by name, and the baristas get a handshake or hug.

When I walked by him on my return trip to the counter, he flashed a number stuck to his palm—the code for the restrooms. His self-appointed job is to greet you and give you the restroom code. Since I was then on my second venti-size cup of tea, I appreciated his service!

He was there every morning that week, always following the same ritual. Move the chair over, turn it around to face out, place his coffee on the now relocated table next to him, and greet everyone in the vicinity.

This dear man was a *participant* in the coffee shop while I hid away as an *observer*. There I was, happy in the corner, left alone, unnoticed. And he all but thrust himself into the community.

The best life, the life God wants us to live, is one of deep and rich relationships—with God first and then grace-filled, honest, and mutually encouraging relationships with others. Some of us will naturally turn our chairs in and some will turn them out, but all of us must learn to open up our tables to at least a few others.

In a fallen world, it's not easy to be committed to relationships, knowing they can break our hearts. For many, this pain and betrayal can begin in their family of origin; all they've known of family is disappointment, abuse, or judgment. Others have had their lives assaulted by early childhood bullying, romantic betrayal, workplace politicking, and the like. Sometimes hurtful church relationships cause people to reject the church. Because relationships can be intensely hurtful at times, it's tempting to give up and isolate ourselves as we go watch movies of other people in dysfunctional relationships, thereby becoming passive observers. Spiritual health calls us to intentionally dismantle isolation and choose to learn the profound satisfaction that comes from being who God made us to be—members of a community blessed with rich relationships.

The triune God who exists in community is best known in community. Stanley Grenz writes, "The image of God is primarily a relational concept. Ultimately we do not reflect God's image on our own but in relationship. Thus the *imago Dei* [image of God] is not primarily what we are as individuals. Rather, it is present among humans in relationship. In a word, the image of God is found in human community."[1]

We were made in God's image to be active, relational daughters and sons, to cocreate, to bring about change, and to be active participants in God's kingdom. The only part of creation that God declared to be "*not* good" was Adam being alone (Genesis 2:18, emphasis added).

We need relationships.

## TURNING YOUR CHAIR OUT

As an introvert, I don't want to suggest that introverts are spiritually deficient, but there *is* a certain relational abundance in turning your chair *out* instead of *in*. I know I need my time alone, but I must learn

I also need time in community (just as extroverts must learn they need some time in solitude). What feels comfortable and safe isn't always the healthiest choice. I need quiet, solitary space to write, but if I never move my chair out, I'll write from a place of mere observation instead of participation, which will affect the way I write, what I write, and what I'm passionate about. Writing without relating is a highway to hell; it's pontificating out of ambition instead of out of love.

I've seen this online. Virulent critics who lack love create many hurtful corners on the internet. They live lives of screaming, derision, and criticizing rather than loving, encouraging, and blessing. We can focus so much on negative observation without healthily relating to people that we can become pharisaical monsters of condemnation, assuming the worst of everybody. Community with worship creates compassion, not judgment.

If you are looking for slights or creatively assuming the worst of what people think, you will find much to condemn. Some of what you are saying may even be true, but you may be manipulating that truth to lift yourself up and destroy others rather than bring light and redemption. You start to look for darkness and even hunt for darkness because you enjoy attacking darkness more than you embrace bringing others into the light.

Teaching without loving and pontificating without helping people is the path well-trodden by the Pharisees. They observed and condemned but never loved. They would be bloggers, podcasters, and political pontificators today. The more I encounter hurting, confused, and struggling people at our church, the less inclined I am to give even ten seconds to the scalp hunting that happens on social media.

While I was at first amazed by the Starbucks customer's audacity—rearranging the furniture to put himself at the center—I became inspired by the role he played in the community, the way he helped make it a community. It became a metaphor for me as I work to unlearn my tendency to isolate instead of participate. This is the question I ask myself whenever I'm in the community: *Am I turning my chair in or out?*

Do you *make* communities, or do you *hide* from community? Does your community encourage, bless, and lift up, or does it go to war, attack, and tear down?

Even if God made you to be an introvert, he didn't make you to be a hermit. He created you to love and be loved, to bless and be blessed. The abundant life is found in abundant *connection*, as Paul stated in 1 Thessalonians 5:11: "Therefore encourage one another and build each other up." You may not realize you need connection, but you do. My wife and I know a young woman whose health had dropped precipitously until a healthcare provider pointed out she was woefully deficient in vitamin D. That changed everything. She didn't know she needed vitamin D, but she did—desperately.

Lonely people sometimes don't realize they need connection, but they do. And desperately so.

## SAMSON AND DAVID

Loving real people, crying with real people, confessing to real people, and hearing their confessions too—this is the life of participation we are created to live. That's why I love being a pastor in a local church and also a writer. Walking with people through life cultivates compassion in me. I'm invited to hear the stories behind the devastation—the hurt that led to the sin, the ache that fertilized an addiction. I become much less prone to judge and far more eager to encourage, bless, and cry tears of understanding instead of screaming an angry, "How dare you!"

Every successful addiction program stresses the need for strong community. It's the whole point of meetings. One meeting won't cure you. A week of meetings won't fix you. It's not until meetings become a new and treasured part of your life that you rewire your brain, soften your heart, and redirect your soul's thirst to find freedom and spiritual abundance. One pill can make you immediately high—and imprison you. One meeting is but the first step in a marathon to the finish line of freedom. Part of unlearning isolation is unlearning the demand for immediate gratification. Gratification is instantaneous ("make me feel numb"); participation is a process ("walk with me on the journey"). But it's the process that helps us slowly grow toward wholeness.

Have you ever noticed how gratification and isolation go hand in hand? If you have a drinking problem, it's quite likely you're usually drinking alone. If you have an issue with food, you go off by yourself and hide the evidence so no one will see. If you're into porn or affairs, you seek out places where you can't be seen. Sin and isolation are soulmates, as are holiness and community.

If meetings and relationships are so essential to overcoming addictions of all kinds, might they not be equally effective to stave off an addiction before it begins?

In his book *Samson and the Pirate Monks*, Nate Larkin notes that in one sense, the biblical figures Samson and David had much in common—two men called by God at an early age, and two men who had radical failures (both involving lust for women). Yet one (Samson) ended up dead in a pile of rubble, becoming a tragic rather than an inspirational figure. Though Samson took out much of the Philistines' leadership, Israel was still under the Philistines' oppressive rule at his death. David emerged from his collapse victorious and commended, and he left behind a legacy on behalf of an entire nation.

Larkin suggests that one reason David and Samson started off as failures but David had a much different ending is that David pursued a life of companionship instead of isolation. Apart from Samson's parents, the only friend we read about in his life wasn't much of a friend; it was his betrayer, Delilah.

By contrast, David had Jonathan. He also drew men whose "names and descriptions . . . go on for pages."[2] These men risked their lives for him, refused to abandon him, and followed him to the desert and into battle.

When chains and darkness encircled him, "Samson didn't call out for help, because he knew there was no one within earshot who cared."[3] He was utterly on his own. For David, "Even as he tumbled headlong into a private hell, David could still see his friends, and his friends could see him. And though he was too weak and confused to call out for help, his friends could see that he was in trouble, and they came to get him."[4] Among those friends was the prophet Nathan who confronted David ("You are the man!" [2 Samuel 12:7]), led him to repentance, and pointed him in a new direction. May God give all of us those kinds of friends!

If you live as Samson lived, utterly alone, you are likely to die as Samson died—utterly alone.

## TWO-WAY RELATIONSHIPS

Pause for a moment, and you'll see that this world, run by powers hostile to God, is a factory that produces loneliness on a global scale. You can have a tough day that didn't feature blatant sin but still produced loneliness. A relationship with a child, parent, spouse, friend, or coworker drained you. Something you cleaned got messed up, making you feel unappreciated. Something you created was ignored or criticized. Urgent distractions kept you from doing what you wanted to do or were supposed to do. A nagging headache, a sore back, weather that deteriorated just when you wanted to go out for a walk or run, a needy individual sucking the last remaining vestiges of your joy—all of this and more can produce a steady hum of frustration that makes you want to *escape*.

The opportunities to escape are abundant—eating, drinking, drugging, gambling, mindless social media scrolling, or endless television streaming. Never in the history of the world have there been so many sparkling trinkets that distract us from lives of faith, worship, and fellowship. Here's what we must learn: Instead of *escape*, we need *refreshment*. As an introvert, my *mind* can be refreshed by sitting out on our deck reading a good novel, with the Big Dry Creek nearby and the Rocky Mountains in the distance. There's a place for that kind of solitude. But my *spirit* needs to be refreshed in worship and fellowship. And we need the worship for our fellowship to be worthwhile.

In his writings, Watchman Nee occasionally played loose with Scripture, but I find his writings about refreshing one another to be quite astute. I want to give him credit for these insights without endorsing all of his other views. Nee pointed out that living in the world tarnishes us.[5] Necessary earthly duties wear us down and make us forget about the spiritual abundance we enjoy in Christ. They can cast a dark cloud over our spirits. It's just a fact of life. "But how good it is if on the road home we meet a brother with an overflowing heart, fresh from communion with God!"[6]

Community calls us back to the abundant life. When you're down, the Spirit of God in me can lift you up. When I'm down, the Spirit of God in you can lift me up. That's why community is so essential to an abundant life. We need to remind each other to take hold of it daily. This can be done directly or indirectly with a smile, a kind word of hope and encouragement, a timely text or email, or a listening ear.

If we purposely live lives of isolation, we're assuming we will never need a pick-me-up. And we're also assuming our limited love for God and way of relating to him give us the only glimpse of God we'll ever need. That's like choosing one item at a buffet—the bread, for example—and looking down at the "fools" who fill their plates with a variety of abundant dishes.

For years my spiritual disciplines included Bible study, prayer, spiritual reading, and intermittent fasting. Later in life, I added spiritual conversation. There are a few people I intentionally talk to on a regular basis. Speaking with them often feels like a spiritual shower, and I exit the conversation feeling cleansed, renewed, inspired, and refreshed. *Not always* though. Sometimes it's just a talk. We shouldn't place too high expectations on any aspect of life. Some runs are better than others; some parties are more enjoyable than others; some personal interactions are more edifying than others, *even with the same people*. But we are made to do two things: to worship God in his beauty and glory and to participate in fellowship, which allows us to refresh others and allows us to be refreshed by others. I'm trying to be more intentional about laying hold of this glorious spiritual practice of fellowship.

Our relationships need to be more than just one-way, where we're always doing the refreshing or always being refreshed. Paul urges us to be mutual encouragers. Spiritually, we can give by receiving, by letting someone else refresh us. If we don't, that relationship might be tainted by pride and self-righteousness. One of my closest friends (for more than twenty years now) was going through a difficult season that was going on for an agonizingly long time. When we talked, the counsel I kept repeating was, "Keep fighting. Don't give up. Stay in the battle." He referred to that advice several times over our next few calls. A few weeks later, a trio of spiritual blasts came my way that made my head spin. He called me early one Friday morning, with God's good words for each of the three issues, laced with Scripture and delivered with passion.

Have you ever been enormously hungry and couldn't think about anything else until you ate a healthy meal, and then after the meal you felt like a new person? That's what spiritual conversation is like with this friend. I was jolted upright, strengthened, and cheered on in the journey of faith with renewed passion and resolve.

Therapy and counseling, while helpful in and of themselves, can't replace connection. Sermons can't compensate for engaging with others. *Refreshing engagement must be mutual*, in which we both give and receive. That's what we are created to do—not to be mere observers, but to be *participants*.

No one can be immune from this. Watchman Nee rightfully affirms, "In the Church there exists no superior class of brothers who have no need to be refreshed. It is something every servant of God depends on."[7] Here's my guess: If you are not regularly connecting with other sisters or brothers in Christ, you are regularly connecting with some kind of compensating sin. Maybe it's an alarming, health-assaulting form of escape. Maybe it's judging or gossiping. Maybe it's a fascination with something that shouldn't really matter much. Maybe you're just a mean poster on the internet.

Take a deep breath. Call a friend or fellow Jesus follower. Tell them you're going to send them a copy of this book with this chapter bookmarked and say, "We need to do *this* more often."

Reconnect and be renewed. Dismantle isolation. Learn community.


## CHOOSE RELATIONSHIP

The story of Abram and Lot demonstrates how spiritual and relational abundance is superior to material and comfort abundance. You may recall that as their families grew and needed to divide, Abram gave his nephew Lot the first choice of where to live. Lot made his decision entirely on material abundance and personal comfort:

> Lot looked around and saw that the whole plain of the Jordan toward Zoar was well watered, like the garden of the LORD, like the land of Egypt. (This was before the LORD destroyed Sodom and Gomorrah.) So Lot chose for himself the whole plain of the Jordan and set out toward the east. The two men parted company: Abram lived in the land of Canaan, while Lot lived among the cities of the plain and pitched his tents near Sodom. Now the people of Sodom were wicked and were sinning greatly against the LORD. (Genesis 13:10–13)

Lot's choice of material abundance over relationship—putting priority on the riches of the land ("well watered, like the garden of the LORD") over the kind of people he'd be living among ("wicked and . . . sinning greatly against the LORD")—imperiled his daughters and led to his wife's death. He also lost all material abundance, since the "well-watered garden" would be turned into a fiery cauldron.

How many marriages have been destroyed by spouses choosing material well-being over relational connection and they end up losing *both*? They work long hours, around the wrong kind of people, until their primary human relationship breaks. They chose some *thing* over some *one*, and it cost them dearly as they had to split up half of what they owned and ignored each other to acquire.

The reason we must learn to value connection over things and lifestyle is that without it, we're liable to sabotage our own happiness and spiritual health. No house can compete with an emotionally connected marriage or compensate for the lack thereof.

A Harvard study begun in 1938 led to "the surprising finding . . . that our relationships and how happy we are in our relationships has a powerful influence on our health." Thus writes Robert Waldinger, director of the study, a psychiatrist at Massachusetts General Hospital and a professor of psychiatry at Harvard Medical School. When it comes to longevity, Waldinger says, "Taking care of your body is important, but tending to your relationships is a form of self-care too. That, I think, is the revelation."[8]

This study confirms scientifically what the Bible tells us by revelation—the most abundant life is a life of abundant connection with others.

> Close relationships, more than money or fame, are what keep people happy throughout their lives, the study revealed. Those ties protect people from life's discontents, help to delay mental and physical decline, and are better predictors of long and happy lives than social class, IQ, or even genes. That finding proved true across the board among both the Harvard men [the original students whose health was tracked] and the inner-city participants [added to the study in the 1970s].[9]

The study determined that "the people who were most satisfied in their relationships at age 50 were the healthiest at age 80." So for your total health and well-being, instead of just focusing on your cholesterol and high blood pressure, focus on your marriage and friendships. Daily exercise is wonderful, but living a lonely life is to your mental and spiritual health what smoking and a sedentary lifestyle are to your lungs.

Since the study initially focused on longevity and health, early researchers didn't concentrate on the need for social connection. "'When the study began, nobody cared about empathy or attachment,' said George Vaillant [a lead researcher from 1966 to 2004]. 'But the key to healthy aging is relationships, relationships, relationships.'"[10]

In fact, some researchers were surprised to learn that relational satisfaction can be a better predictor of healthy aging than genetics. They also found that those who were "train wrecks" in their twenties or thirties but became relationally connected later on were better off than superhealthy people who became increasingly isolated.

Choose to become connected. If you're married, make your marriage a priority, even if it costs you financially and vocationally. Get involved in your local church; become an active participant instead of merely an attender. We need to bless and be blessed to get the full benefits of relational connection.

Lisa and I have benefited greatly from small groups. We're always on the lookout for compatible friends. I have made it an agenda item to check in with certain friends on a regular basis. If I don't think about and prioritize these relationships, I can go months without talking to some of my closest brothers in Christ. My goal is to have a significant conversation at least once a day—with one of my children, a friend, or a colleague. (Of course, I hope that Lisa and I have a significant conversation every day, so I don't count that, though if we've just been going through the motions for a few days, I want to notice it and address it.)

Do you want to experience a more abundant and fulfilling life? Dismantle isolation. Learn to participate and connect. Turn your chair out instead of in, and embrace God's joy and presence through relational connection.

# 5

# DISMANTLING SELF-CENTERED SALVATION

## Learn the Value of Sacrificial Service

*The kingdom of God is so shockingly opposite the way the rest of the world works that I need constant reminding of what it looks like and how good it is.*

BRANT HANSEN, *UNOFFENDABLE*

A faithful life in Christ depends in large part on your understanding not just the *facts* of Jesus' death but the *point* of Jesus' death. There's a difference between the facts and the point of an event.

Back in the days of the Soviet Union, *Pravda*, the state newspaper, was famous for its stories that might be factually true but were radically misleading. For example, one headline announced, "Soviet Runner Second, American Runner Third from Last."

The race involved just three people, and the American won the race. But first place in a three-person race is, technically speaking, "third from last." So the headline was technically true but wildly deceptive. The facts missed the point that the American defeated both the Soviet runner and the other runner.

When she was in high school, journalist, writer, and filmmaker Nora Ephron* took a journalism class in which the teacher gave an assignment to write the lede to a story as a way to help the students distinguish between the facts and the point. The teacher introduced the assignment by presenting the story's relevant facts:

Kenneth I. Peters, the principal of Beverly Hills High School, announced today that the entire high school faculty will travel to Sacramento next Thursday for a colloquium in new teaching methods. Among the speakers will be anthropologist Margaret Mead, college president Dr. Robert Maynard Hutchins, and California governor Edmund "Pat" Brown.[1]

With that information, the professor asked the journalism students to write the lede. One suggested, "Margaret Mead, Maynard Hutchins, and Governor Brown will address the faculty on . . ."

But that was wrong.

Another started out, "Next Thursday, the high school faculty will . . ."

Wrong again.

The teacher proceeded to unveil the true lede: "There will be no school Thursday."

For journalists, the lede refers not just to the facts but also to the *point* of the facts. With all the faculty out, the school can't hold classes.

---

* Nora's many movies include *You've Got Mail*, *When Harry Met Sally*, *Silkwood*, and *Sleepless in Seattle*.

What the students most need to know and want to know is that they don't have to go to school that day.

If we know the facts about Jesus' death at Golgotha but miss the point, we risk, in the words of C. S. Lewis, "running about with fire extinguishers whenever there is a flood."[2]

One of the reasons we're running around with fire extinguishers during a flood is that we don't understand the lede about Jesus' death. We get the facts right, but the point is wrong. We need to rethink what the point really is so we can learn what really matters.

Before we go on, ask yourself, *What is the proper lede for the events of Good Friday that culminate with Jesus' death on the cross at Golgotha?*

## A FALSE LEDE

Here is perhaps the most popular false lede about Golgotha. Every word in the following sentence is true, but it misses the point.

---

Jesus lived a perfect life, died on a cross, and rose
from the dead so that our sins could be forgiven
and we could live with him in heaven.

---

Take a closer look at Golgotha. Jesus demonstrates the lede for us by how he refuses to respond to cruel taunts. Amid the most beautiful, glorious, and magnificent accomplishment in the history of the world—one that will never be surpassed—people mocked Jesus as he was being crucified: "Come down from the cross, if you are the Son of God!" (Matthew 27:40).

Talk about restraint! These people are saying to Jesus, "Prove your power. Why would you stay up there if you didn't have to?" In their minds, Jesus' refusal to back away from overwhelming suffering proves that he couldn't.

But here's the truth: Jesus wouldn't come down from the cross because he was (and is) the Son of God. Staying on the cross to finish his work was *proof* of his divinity, not a refutation of it.

The old way of thinking that must be dismantled is this: "Why do something that hurts? It makes no sense. Prove you're superior by doing what's best for *you*."

In fact, Jesus proved he was superior by doing what was best for *us*, not for *him*, demonstrating that he looks at life and obedience in a drastically different way than we do.

Everyone watching the crucifixion knew the facts: Jesus was being tortured, and in a physical sense his life was rapidly coming to an end. Only Jesus understood the point. Jesus is the only one to whom it made sense that he should stay on the cross instead of abandoning it, which he could have done. That reality points us to the true lede of Golgotha.

## A TRUE LEDE

Here's a lede that looks beyond individual comfort and explains why Jesus endured the scorn, shame, and torture of the cross:

---

Jesus died so that we would all live as he lived—not for our own interests, but to advance the kingdom of God.

---

I didn't come up with this lede. The apostle Paul did. I'm merely paraphrasing what Paul wrote in 2 Corinthians 5:15: "He died for all, that those who live should no longer live for themselves but for him who died for them and was raised again."

That is the point of Jesus' death—no longer living for ourselves but for Jesus. Following the sacrifice and resurrection of Jesus, God sent his Holy Spirit to empower us in order that we might participate in his sovereign work to remake and reorder a fallen world. We live a life of worship and sacrificial service as he brings forth his new kingdom. That's the *full* gospel.

Jesus died not just so you could go to heaven, but also so you would bring heaven to earth. What we need to dismantle and then learn is this: Life isn't about securing *personal comfort in eternity*; life is about fulfilling our *divine mission on earth*. That's the *point* of Golgotha.

The headline:

Jesus died on the cross and rose from the dead.

The lede:

Jesus died so that we would all live as he lived.

The point:

God is remaking the world through the sacrifice and resurrection of Jesus and has sent his Holy Spirit to empower us to participate in building his new kingdom.

# THE GOSPEL BEFORE THE CROSS

For those who think the gospel is summarized as "Jesus lived a perfect life, died on a cross, and rose from the dead to forgive our sins and open the way for us to live with him in heaven," consider Luke 9:6: "[The disciples] set out and went from village to village, *proclaiming the good news [the gospel]* and healing people everywhere" (emphasis added).

When the disciples were preaching, Jesus was still very much alive. The disciples couldn't have preached about the cross or Jesus' resurrection. What was "the gospel" if they weren't talking about those facts we often see as constituting the entire gospel?

In Luke 9:2 we read, "[Jesus] sent them out to proclaim the kingdom of God and to heal the sick." Remember, this is prior to Jesus' death. What, then, were they proclaiming? Namely, this—a new world has come! God is calling the world back from rebellion and hatred toward worship and love. Our call is to now advance God's kingdom—his influence, his reign—instead of living simply for ourselves. Our task is to turn people to live for God instead of for themselves.

If we make personal salvation the lede ("trust in Jesus so you can be saved"), we miss the point. The statement is true, but it's not the full gospel. It's focused on self. Jesus died to make us kingdom-centered. So the distorted facts of the incomplete gospel read like a *Pravda* headline proclaiming that the winning runner is actually third from last. It's a true deception.

Here's what we must dismantle—our definition of the gospel as primarily "God will *save* us" as we go on to embrace the more complete statement "God will *enlist* us." Our sermons tend to be centered more on "Christ died for us" than "we must live for God."

Both are true, of course. Both are essential and glorious—and Christ's death is a necessary precondition of the other. Christ *did* die for us (let's worship him forever!), but the point is that he did so *in order that* we can live for God.

## DRAFTED

Knowing the true point of the gospel helps me accept my place in God's work with humility. It frees me from the crushing burdens of being jealous of others and feeling unappreciated. Why? Because I'm embracing the truth that God's work isn't about me; it's about him! When I live like this, I'm not even thinking about what people are thinking of me.

I'm a lifelong football fan—college football first, pro football second. I even like to watch the pro football draft. It's exciting to see young men achieve lifelong dreams. There's a helpful analogy here.

Every draft selection is for a purpose. Each player is chosen not just to be on the team (i.e., get into heaven), but to play a particular position. If you see a player who is five ten, 160 pounds, you know he's not being drafted to play offensive lineman. He's almost certainly a punter or kicker. If a player is 325 pounds, he's not going to play cornerback.

When God drafts us, he has a role in mind, far more than us just wearing the team jersey for eternity. He's not selecting us to sit on the bench and cash a paycheck. There's a position he wants us to play.

With that analogy, here's what we must learn: Jesus didn't die just so that your soul would be *saved*; he died so that your life would be *invested*. The glory of the moment isn't putting on the jersey on Friday night draft night; it's stepping onto the field on Saturday or Sunday afternoon and doing your job.

Life in Jesus is far more radical than most of us realize. Dying to self and rising to service causes offense for many in our world today. The failure to understand the need to unlearn this self-first dynamic makes difficult passages sound more problematic than they are. Take Titus 2:9–10, for example: "Teach slaves to be subject to their masters in everything, to try to please them, not to talk back to them, and not to steal from them, but to show that they can be fully trusted."

If you only read the headline but miss the lede and the point, this will anger and offend you. How dare Paul talk about slavery like this? Out of context, it sounds like he was condoning it. Why didn't he tell slaves to rebel? Why didn't he organize the church into a first-century emancipation organization? For starters, the social structure supporting slavery at the time might have made that strategy lethal for slaves.

In the book of Philemon, Paul told an owner that his slave was a brother, not a servant, and he should be set free. Proclaiming to a believing slave owner that a slave must be freed demonstrated in this context that Paul believed that owning someone was inconsistent with following Christ.

But for our purposes here, when we get the lede and the point, we understand what comes next. Paul's primary purpose in writing this command to Titus was revealed in the fifteen words that occur at the end of verse 10—the point revealed in Paul's "so that": *so that in every way they will make the teaching about God our Savior attractive* (emphasis added).

Paul wasn't primarily concerned about his readers' comfort or even their freedom, but rather about the advancement of God's kingdom. Admittedly, this is scandalous to our sense of personal justice. Everything Paul wrote about marriage, parenting, gender roles, lawsuits, and church order falls under this same rubric—what will advance God's kingdom the most? Individual comfort, rights, and privileges cannot compete with Paul's passion to heed Jesus' words in the Sermon on the Mount: "Seek *first* [God's] kingdom" (Matthew 6:33, emphasis added).

I don't want us to minimize the importance, glory, and good news of salvation. Far from it. I just want us to learn to marry salvation and service so we don't miss the point of salvation. The genius of Paul's thought is that he married salvation and service—not service *to be* saved (which is why we often undervalue the notion of service), but service *because* we are saved.

If we want a brilliant faith and a brilliant church, we must marry salvation and service. Some churches and denominations focus on one, and some on the other: "The gospel is about salvation"; "the gospel is about service." Both positions are true, but not exclusively.

Service doesn't save us. But salvation doesn't sideline us. We're not saved just because we serve. But we should question our salvation if there is no service.

## COME DOWN FROM THAT CROSS!

Why is self-centered salvation so important to dismantle and others-centered service so important to learn?

If you are God's child, the day will come when some people will say, "Come down from that cross!" and think they're doing you a favor.

In your pain or predicament, some of Jesus' words may seem harsh to you. They may seem to undercut your immediate happiness and push you toward discomfort, perhaps even guilt. Though our Lord couldn't have been clearer—"Whoever does not take up their cross and follow me is not worthy of me" (Matthew 10:38)—they will say to you, "God loves you so much that he *must* want you to come down from the cross."

Self-centered salvation compels you to see God's will through the lens of personal benefit, entitlement, and personal comfort. There was no personal benefit to Jesus on the cross. There was no sense of entitlement that could keep him on the cross. There was no comfort bleeding out of him as he died on that cross. The cross had nothing to do with his own salvation.

But he stayed on it all the same out of his commitment to serve.

A physician told me about the challenges she faces as a general practitioner these days. Sometimes she feels that her office spends just as much time fighting insurance companies and wrangling over inadequate Medicaid reimbursement as they do treating patients. To meet her expenses, she often sees fifty patients in a day. She graduated from med school in her thirties with hundreds of thousands of dollars in student loan debt, but because she is a doctor, everyone assumes she is rich, entitled, and privileged. They suggest she should only be making less than half of what she earns or should even work for free. After all, what kind of Christian seeks to profit off the illnesses of others?

This particular spin on her motives is grotesque, but it gets worse. Many of her patients go onto WebMD before the appointment and already have diagnosed themselves and talk condescendingly to her if she disagrees. They'll question her credentials, imply that she has sold out to Big Pharma, and threaten her with one-star reviews. And then there are the clever drug addicts who know how to present certain symptoms to get painkillers and will respond with dreadful anger if they don't get the prescription they want.

On top of all that, if she makes one mistake or misses one diagnosis (remember, she's seeing dozens of patients a day), she's likely to be sued for millions of dollars and threatened with the revocation of her license to practice medicine.

It would be easy for her to think, *I don't need this!* and just walk away. She's doing a good work but is accused of operating out of bad motives. She willingly exposes herself to all kinds of pathogens but is accused of being selfish.

Who could blame her for wanting to come down off that cross? She's a well-educated person. She could do better. She could perhaps be happier and less frustrated and work fewer hours—except this is what she is convinced God has called her to do, along with the four weeks a year she volunteers at a medical mission overseas (even for this some accuse her of having a white savior complex).

If you're a Christ follower who knows God has called you to do what you're doing, you won't listen to the crowds that tempt you with, "Come down from that cross." Instead, you'll listen to Paul's words to Timothy: "Endure hardship . . . discharge all the duties of your ministry" (2 Timothy 4:5).

Teachers, coaches, police officers, child protective services workers, pastors, and the like, take note. Just because the pay is low and the expectations high, and the people you serve are as likely to resent you as appreciate you and may even try to sue you instead of paying you, it doesn't mean you should jump off the cross. If the point of Golgotha is my eternal destiny, my cross isn't relevant. I can come down from it and nothing is lost. But if you understand the lede of Golgotha, instead of saying, "You're right, I should come down from this cross" you'll say, "No, I cannot do that. I belong to God, and that's why I bear this cross."

Without grasping the point of Golgotha, I'll think, *This hurts, and it must stop. If I'm not celebrated, I'll go elsewhere. If my rights aren't respected, I'll move on.*

With the point of Golgotha firmly established, I'll think, *Jesus told me to take up my cross daily and follow him. Just because I'm getting tired of the same old cross doesn't mean I should come down from it.*

If you live primarily for yourself, you are not living the Christian life. I'm not saying you're not a Christian. That's for God to determine. I am saying, definitively, that you are not currently living the Christian life as Jesus and Paul define it.

You have been called to something bigger, more glorious, and ultimately far more fulfilling than simply resting in your own salvation and certainly than building your own kingdom. Whether your kingdom is centered around personal wealth, romance, comfort, family, or retirement, if it's primarily *your* kingdom, you're missing the mark. You were made for more than that kingdom. All of us are called to seek first the kingdom of God (Matthew 6:33).

## NO SMALL MATTER

To *know* the truth but not *live* the truth is one of the greatest tragedies of all time. That's why it's tragic when Christians don't understand the right lede.

William Law warned, "There is nothing more . . . to be dreaded than the neglect of our Christian calling; which is not to serve the little uses of a short life, but to redeem souls unto God, to fill heaven with saints, and finish a kingdom of eternal glory unto God."[3]

Jesus didn't go to Golgotha just so you'd go to church on Sunday morning and give a little bit of your money in the offering plate. He claims your *life*—all of it. We must live entirely different lives. A Dallas pastor spoke of an older woman in his congregation who kept working well into her seventies. It wasn't to pay off a mortgage (that was already paid for); it wasn't to go to Europe (she never left Texas). It was to support fourteen Compassion kids.

Paul Buursma was born in 1983 with a hole in his diaphragm. The doctors gave him just a 2 percent chance of surviving infancy at that time, given the critical nature of his condition. And yet Paul lived to be thirty-two years old.

Thirty-two very good years.

In a wheelchair. Facing the impacts of cerebral palsy and a lifelong restrictive lung disease.

He volunteered at Goodwill, worked the dining hall and campus store at Calvin University, had a stint as a greeter at Russ' Restaurant, and welcomed visitors to the local children's museum and the world-renowned Frederik Meijer Gardens & Sculpture Park.

But more importantly, he had a heart brimming with God's love and an ear-to-ear smile for everyone who would pause and interact with him. The celebration of his life following his death was a true celebration. Paul wrenched every opportunity from the limitations he was given and lived a life of service to God and others. I've met plenty of people who would be singularly focused to the point of obsession: "Get me out of this chair!"

Paul Buursma's plea was different: "Father, keep me in your will."

I don't know what your cross is, but I know what your calling is. You don't have to be "healthy" to serve God. You don't have to be particularly talented. You don't have to be rich or smart or unusually holy. You just have to be *available*. You must believe that the full gospel isn't just about going to heaven; it's about all of us opening our hearts so that God can display the power of heaven on earth through us as he remakes the world.

That's why I believe how you define "the gospel" is one of the most important tasks you will ever undertake. You may need to dismantle prior understandings and learn what the apostle Paul and Paul Buursma leaned into. Thousands of summer camps across the United States seek to get their young campers saved—and I say good for them!

But how many are seeking to get them *enlisted*? Isn't that what it means to become a disciple?

# PAUSE

Pause for just a moment. It's very likely that something in your life at this very moment feels like a cross, and it's just as likely that someone is saying, "Come down from that cross!" Maybe you're the one saying it. Maybe half of your prayers have been, "God, take me down from this cross."

What are you going to do with this new lede?

Are you going to come down from the cross just because it hurts?

Ask yourself, *What am I living for? Is it* my *kingdom, or is it God's?* Consider how you spend your money and your time, and ask yourself, *What gets me excited?* Are you living what William Law called "the little uses of a short life," or are you trying to "finish a kingdom of eternal glory unto God"?

What's your headline?

What's your lede?

What's your point?

Let's dismantle a self-centered description of the gospel and learn to make the point of the gospel the very thing God's inspired writer of Scripture called it: "[Jesus] died for all, that those who live should no longer live for themselves but for him who died for them and was raised again" (2 Corinthians 5:15).

# 6

# DISMANTLING THE NEED FOR COMFORT

## *Learn the Value of Adversity*

*Affliction is a fire to purge out our dross, and to
make our graces shine. Affliction is the remedy
which cures all our spiritual diseases.*

THOMAS BROOKS, *PRECIOUS REMEDIES AGAINST SATAN'S DEVICES*

*Before I was afflicted I went astray,
but now I obey your word.*

PSALM 119:67

Last night, a seminary student of mine asked my advice for three different couples she's working with, all of whom face sexual addiction. This morning, I read a friend's book about a long descent into opioid and alcohol addiction and the agonizingly slow climb out of it. I'm in the middle of a long stretch of work (more than two weeks without a day off), which I try to avoid but sometimes fall into, and my addiction of choice is sugar. When I'm overly stressed and tired, when adrenaline has coursed through me during a long engagement and I'm off the stage, my brain *begs* for that sugar rush.

We're all messed up in different ways, but if there's one thing I'm more addicted to than sugar (which Lisa is working on), it's comfort. I crave comfort. I seek comfort. I hate the lack of comfort. Where do I seek comfort? Everywhere! A chair that forms around me, with a footrest at just the right angle. A winter coat that envelops me, shielding me from the wind and the cold. Shoes that fit so well I don't even know they're on my feet. A task undertaken with no interruptions. Relationships with no conflict. Roads with no traffic. Prayer with no boredom. Customer service that is competent. Exercise with minimal pain. Work with no failure.

In fact, life without any complications.

I organize my life in desperate and futile attempts to stay in my comfort zone throughout the day, but God makes my best-laid plans impossible because he loves me.

That last statement—that God makes unbroken comfort impossible because he loves me—is something I've had to learn. The thought that unbroken comfort is a sign of God's blessing and favor is something I've had to dismantle and purge.

There's a significant difference between *enduring* afflictions—sickness, aging, personal attacks, financial hardship, the death of loved ones, persecution—and believing we *need* them. It took me decades before I understood that afflictions are *necessary* for a mature heart and soul. Far from resenting them, as I did for so long, I should be thankful for them. In the words of seventeenth-century Puritan William Gurnall, "God's wounds cure, sin's kisses kill."[1]

J. I. Packer unmasked my spiritual disease: "It is a mistake . . . to imagine that the good for which God works is our unbroken ease and comfort. God's goal is, rather, our sanctification and Christlikeness, the true holiness that is the highway to happiness."[2]

We are abundantly rebellious, which means we must at times be abundantly disciplined, which can be painful. Even this painful element leads to abundance, however. Affliction isn't about God's anger. He does not want to shame us. On the contrary, he intends through this affliction to bless us and enrich us. Some may call this the blessing nobody wants, but God loves us so much he'll give us what we need, even if we resent him for it. He always does what is best for us.

I'm not suggesting all suffering is discipline, but it is just as foolish to suggest that no suffering ever involves discipline as it is to suggest that every act of suffering is discipline. We need afflictions for many reasons, apart from the inevitable effects of living in a fallen world. What I had to unlearn is the mistaken notion that afflictions primarily come because of discipline or punishment. That's just not true. They come to shape us, empower us, reveal God to us, make us more dependent on him, and complete us. "My Father is the gardener. . . . Every branch that does bear fruit he prunes so that it will be even more fruitful" (John 15:1, 2).

Begin the dismantling process that demands 24/7 comfort, and picture yourself as a plant whose gardener is God. He is intensely focused on your welfare—your growth, your protection from noxious weeds, and your fruitfulness. You have all his attention. Nothing will get to you or happen to you that he won't see and respond to. The truth of this chapter is entirely dependent on you seeing God as an active, caring, loving gardener, or shepherd, whichever image draws you most clearly into God's heart and truth.

As William Gurnall reminded us, "As sin kills the sinner laughing, so God saves poor souls weeping and bleeding under the wounds which his word gives them." He speaks of the "happy soul" who, by reading and heeding God's Word, escapes "the enchanting arms of thy lusts that would have kissed thee to death and to fall into the hands of a faithful God," who means no more hurt to us by the suffering he allows "than the saving of thy soul."[3]

My demand for comfort and my resistance to adversity set me up to fall hard and make me vulnerable to all kinds of Satan's schemes—but God will warn me first, catch me if I don't listen and have to pay the price, and then put me back on my feet and set me on a new path. God is a master physician who may cut us so we may be healed in the long term. Early surrender may spare us much later suffering.

But not all.

If we don't unlearn the demand for comfort and learn the *need* for adversity, we'll still face adversity, but we'll face it with resentment and doubt toward God, keeping us in a spiritual spiral that can darken a decade or more of our lives.

## MUTE CHRISTIAN UNDER THE SMARTING ROD

The English Puritan preacher Thomas Brooks (1608–1680) was perhaps *the* classic writer who most acutely understood the need for afflictions. His brilliant book *Mute Christian Under the Smarting Rod* helped me dismantle decades of wrong thinking about afflictions and how to face them. I've recommended this book to many hurting souls and have been thanked profusely for doing so.

Brooks's thesis is twofold: Afflictions are necessary, and our best, most spiritually beneficial posture in the face of them is surrendered silence. Wrote Brooks, "It is the great duty and concern of gracious souls to be mute and silent under the greatest afflictions, the saddest providences, and sharpest trials which they meet with in this world."[4]

Let's keep the emphasis on the idea of *surrendered* over Brooks's use of the words *mute* and *silent*. My friend Bill Walkup, an assistant professor at Southwest Baptist University and a licensed counselor, helped me rethink Brooks's emphasis on silence by pointing out the numerous biblical characters who weren't silent—indeed, many psalms and the entire book of Lamentations include numerous verbal protestations. Bill also points out that God doesn't generally call us to silence but rather to communion (i.e., to dialogue). In his counseling practice, Bill has found that enforced silence often leads to bitterness and resentment (think of a parent or an authority figure telling the child or student to shut up, which often results in outward obedience but inward resentment). With these caveats, I found Brooks's charge to be life-changing: "Affliction is a fire to purge out our dross and to make our graces shine. Affliction is the remedy which cures all our spiritual diseases."[5]

When I used to think afflictions weren't necessary, the last thing I did in the face of them was trust God or listen. For me, afflictions didn't lead to dialogue, they led to a whining monologue—mine! Invariably, I tried to pray them away. This will sound so pathetic, arrogant, infantile, and misguided, but it's true: I once even thought that perhaps I could obey my way out of them.

Monstrous, I know.

I had to unlearn the cause of and reasons for afflictions, as well as the proper response.

Afflictions will come to us. We are going to get sick. We are going to be betrayed. We will be persecuted. Some of those we love the most will break our hearts the hardest. We will be treated unfairly and ridiculed. We will be inconvenienced. We will. The only question is whether we will learn to receive these afflictions with the right spirit so we can gain maximum benefit from them.

Many of the classic writers embraced the beautiful brutality of being shaped by suffering. John Calvin wrote, "Whomever the Lord has adopted and deemed worthy of his fellowship ought to prepare themselves for a hard, toilsome, and unquiet life, crammed with very many and various kinds of evil."[6] This quote alone drastically reset my expectations, as I believe it to be true to life. Don't you? When we accept this reality, we lose the bitterness, anxiety, and struggle and can finally yield into the peaceful rest of surrender.

Calvin explains that the Father will treat us the same way he treated the Son:

> For even though that Son was beloved above the rest, and in him the Father's mind was well pleased, yet we see that far from being treated indulgently or softly, to speak the truth, while he dwelt on earth he was not only tried by a perpetual cross but his whole life was nothing but a sort of perpetual cross. The apostle notes the reason: that it behooved him to "learn obedience through what he suffered" (Heb. 5:8).[7]

If Christ accepted his lot of learning obedience through suffering, who are we to object to the same process? Note that Jesus, *the sinless one*, learned obedience from what he suffered. How much more must we, steeped in sin at birth, suffer to learn our obedience?

But here's the rub: Our natural selves value comfort over obedience; at least, I did. In fact, I'm ashamed to admit that one of my motivations to obey was the mistaken notion that it would lead to greater comfort.

This is what I had to dismantle. I thought I might be able to obey my way out of suffering when in fact I needed to learn I must suffer to learn how to obey! Learning the proper perspective doesn't make suffering less painful, but it does make it less bitter. Wrote Calvin, "How much can it do to soften all the bitterness of the cross, that the more we are afflicted with adversities, the more surely our fellowship with Christ is confirmed."[8]

Paul tells us that knowing the power of the resurrection and sharing in Christ's suffering is a package deal (Philippians 3:10–11). Wanting one without the other is like wanting ice cream without the cold sensation.

Do you want power? Then learn to surrender when you suffer.

What matters more than getting *out* of suffering is staying *in* surrender. Don't let afflictions turn your mind or heart from God. Thomas Brooks wrote, "The afflicted soul knows that a righteous God can do nothing but that which is righteous; it knows that God is uncontrollable, and therefore the afflicted man . . . keeps silence before him."[9]

It was such a blessing to read Brooks when a lifelong love looked like it might be taken away from me. I have been a long-distance runner since I was sixteen years old. It helps me deal with stress, keeps me fit, helps me manage a sometimes overly busy and neurotic brain, inspires thoughts, calms me, helps me sleep, helps maintain weight, gets me outdoors, occasionally provides a pleasant runner's high—I could go on, but I think I've made my point.

During a stressful time in my life, I had another bout with plantar fasciitis, a brutally painful foot/heel condition that punishes a person on every step. For me, it usually takes a year or so to overcome it. As soon as that time passed, however, my knees started to hurt. I could barely eke out three miles without feeling like hot coals were living under my kneecaps for the rest of the day.

Forewarned by Brooks, I remembered that *more than I needed to run, I needed to surrender.* Instead of being bitter that God wasn't healing me, I needed a sweet, thankful spirit for all the ways God has blessed me. I didn't want a physical injury to unleash a spiritual one. In fact, I wanted to use my physical weakness to become spiritually stronger.

By God's grace, it happened. When I could run even one lap around Denver's Washington Park (just two and a half miles), with the mountains in the background, I worshiped God. When my knees started screaming before I got halfway around and I had to move into a walk, I still worshiped God. I'm deeply thankful for Brooks's kind counsel before this season hit and a lifelong coping mechanism was taken away.

I hope I can run another marathon someday. But I am desperate to see God's face every day.

Because our faith in God is so intensely relational, we must never forget that just because God's hand seems to be against us, that doesn't mean his *heart* is. God's heart is never against us. In fact, he has a greater interest in us than we have in ourselves.[10]

God's endgame is to draw us ever closer to himself. Satan's endgame is to use affliction to pry us apart from God. Brooks again: "In all the afflictions he brought upon Job, Satan's design was not so much to make Job a beggar—as it was to make him a blasphemer."[11]

Since this is the real temptation, learn to trust instead of murmur. It's fine—even healthy—to voice your hurt, but think humble over haughty. As Brooks wrote, "God is a wise physician, and he would never give strong medicine if a weaker one could effect the cure."[12] Murmuring (choosing contempt over reverence, pride over humility, demand over surrender) is spiritual smoking, overeating, and drunkenness all joined together. It slowly erodes our spiritual health. When we murmur, we're essentially judging God and trying to change his mind. When we trust, we're *listening* to receive God's thoughts and allowing him to change *our* minds. Which do you think is more likely to lead to spiritual health—God changing his mind, or us changing our perspective?

## MAKING THE MOST OF YOUR PAIN

Once I dismantle my demand for unbroken comfort and ease, I need to learn the value of afflictions. This begins with believing that in these struggles, God is at work for our good, as Scripture tells us (Romans 8:28–29).

Thomas Brooks lists many of afflictions' benefits:[13]

- Being afflicted opens my eyes so I can "come to have a clearer sight of my sins and of myself, and a fuller sight of my God, Job 33:27, 28; 40:4, 5; 13:1–7."
- Afflictions can help "kill my sins, and soften my heart."
- Through afflictions, "the Lord will crucify my heart more and more to the world, and the world to my heart, Gal. 6:14; Psalm 131:1–3."
- Afflictions will foster humility and "keep pride from my soul, Job 33:14–21. Surely these afflictions are but the Lord's pruning-knives, by which he will bleed my sins, and prune my heart, and make it more fertile and fruitful; they are but the Lord's portion, by which he will clear me, and rid me of those spiritual diseases and maladies, which are most deadly and dangerous to my soul! Affliction is such a potion, as will carry away all soul-diseases, better than all other remedies, Zech. 13:8, 9."
- Painful afflictions can increase pleasurable "spiritual experiences" as well as help me become a "partaker of God's holiness, Heb. 12:10. As black soap makes white clothes, so does sharp afflictions make holy hearts."
- God reveals himself to me in my afflictions and "will fix my soul more than ever upon the great [importance] of the eternal world, John 14:1–3; Rom. 8:17, 18; 2 Cor. 4:16–18."

- Afflictions train me to become a more effective minister. "By these afflictions the Lord will work in me more tenderness and compassion toward those who are afflicted, Heb. 10:34; 13:3."

An example of this: I discovered I had keratoconus, a degenerative eye disease, in my late twenties. I never had it treated because the treatment back then involved a cornea transplant and I never got on the list. According to my eye doctor, my brain has learned to operate with the use of just one eye, which is fine (though a bit of a hassle when I'm biking and have a difficult time looking over my shoulder). One of our daughters began to experience the same symptoms in her twenties and got right on it. Not only did the new treatment stop the progression, but she was also among the blessed 20 percent who saw improvement in her eyesight. With glasses, she may even get back to twenty-twenty vision.

The reason she jumped on it and was even aware of its existence is that her father had suffered through it. In a very real sense, my suffering kept her from suffering the same lifelong consequences. If my having keratoconus came at the price of our daughter having received treatment early on and not having to suffer from it, it's a price I'd gladly pay, as practically every parent would.

What if all of our afflictions have a similar effect—if by our suffering, others are warned or helped or instructed?

In light of all this, Thomas Brooks goes beyond saying afflictions are necessary to calling them "God's love-tokens."[14]

Let's review this unlearning and relearning, without all the quotes and flowery language, so that you can burn into your mind the good that comes from afflictions and become convinced that you need suffering. Affliction:

- gives us a clearer vision of our sins, ourselves, and our God

- kills sins
- softens our heart
- removes us from worldly influence
- attacks pride and fosters humility
- increases pleasurable "spiritual experiences"
- helps us grow in holiness
- reveals God to us
- fixes our thoughts on eternity
- equips us to minister to others who are afflicted

Which one of these benefits do we *not* need? Which one of them can be obtained without passing through some form of affliction?

God's "love-tokens" indeed! Knowing how beneficial our afflictions are, perhaps we can better surrender to them. Brooks one more time: "*What God wills is best*, Heb. 12:10. When he wills sickness, sickness is better than health; when he wills weakness, weakness is better than strength; when he wills want, want is better than wealth; when he wills reproach, reproach is better than honour; when he wills death, death is better than life."[15]

Again, it all comes back to viewing God as a caring, profoundly involved parent overseeing our welfare.

## WHAT OUR CROSSES DO

John Calvin adds to Brooks's list with a few of his own:*

1. "The cross leads us to perfect trust in God's power."[16]

   Without suffering we cling to "stupid and empty confidence

---

* Of course, Calvin was born a century before Brooks. I'm not saying that Calvin is building on Brooks's insights but that he is adding to our reflections here.

in the flesh" rather than live lives of humility and dependence on God. When pride begins to reign, God "afflicts us either with disgrace or poverty, or bereavement, or disease, or other calamities."

We resent afflictions in exact proportion to our ignorance of our pride and our blindness to pride's spiritual devastation. We think we're patient, until God gives us something that tries our patience. We think we can forgive, until we are asked to forgive an act so heinous that we realize we just can't do it on our own. We think we are strong until we are faced with a temptation that overwhelms us.

Need I go on? We *think*, but God *knows*, and he uses afflictions to *reveal* to us what he already knows and we don't.

2. "The cross permits us to experience God's faithfulness and gives us hope for the future."[17]

   How do we really know that God will provide for us in our needs unless he allows us to really need him?

3. "The cross [serves] as medicine."[18]

   It's a sad reality of life that we tend to be "corrupted by [our] indulgence" and need affliction to bring us back, in the same way that it's just plain healthy to go for a walk after we eat a heavy meal. God is a master physician and knows just what kinds of afflictions to prescribe for each individual believer. Receiving blessing upon blessing tends to make us spiritually bloated. Affliction is the necessary exercise that keeps us healthy.

4. "The cross [serves] as fatherly chastisement."[19]

   Discipline is *mercy*. "In the very harshness of tribulations we must recognize the kindness and generosity of our Father toward us, since he does not even then cease to promote our salvation. For he afflicts us not to ruin or destroy us but, rather, to free us from the condemnation of the world."

5. "Bearing the cross . . . [is] suffering for righteousness' sake."[20]

It is impossible to live a righteous life in an unrighteous world and not be persecuted. Jesus told us the world will *hate* us (John 15:19). Hatred motivates people to harm us, even as love motivates us to serve others. In this sense, the crosses don't always help us, but they are inevitable in a world that opposes God.

John Calvin and Thomas Brooks agreed that accepting our need for afflictions doesn't turn us into stoics who act as if we just don't care. We still hurt. We still cry. We still pour out laments to God. We grieve and groan. We even pray for deliverance. We may scream, "Put me back in that comfortable chair. Put me back in those comfortable shoes."

What we must not do is forget our need for afflictions. What we must not do is fail to surrender. We don't have to be a stoic, but we do strive to stay God's servants who understand their place in his kingdom, God's children who embrace their place in God's family.

I hate afflictions, but I love what they do. That's what I had to dismantle and then learn.

## PROSPERITY AND PROBLEMS

I don't want my reflections in this chapter to cause Christians to become suspicious of or feel guilty about comfort, affluence, and honor. God brings us through both blessings and afflictions, and surrender means we accept either one at his direction.

Thomas Brooks taught that a maturing believer needs times of both prosperity and challenge: "The life of a Christian is filled up with interchanges of sickness and health, weakness and strength, want and wealth, disgrace and honour, crosses and comforts, miseries and mercies, joys and sorrows, mirth and mourning; all honey would harm us; all wormwood would undo us—a composition of both is the best way in the world to keep our souls in a healthy constitution."[21]

Don't feel guilty when God blesses you and honors you. Receive it gratefully and joyfully. But don't feel bitter when God breaks you and seems to bring you down. Surrender to both. Worship God in both. Maintain an even-keeled faith in both. Both blessings and afflictions are likely to give way to the other in due season.

It is not wrong or immature to pray to be delivered from our afflictions as long as we maintain a surrendered heart in the midst of them. Jesus prayed for the cup of his suffering to be removed; when his request was refused, he asked again. And then again (Matthew 26:39–44). After the third refusal, he drank from it. That's our model.

Bill Walkup (mentioned earlier in the chapter) told me that in his practice, he sees three types of response to adversity. The first type lies down in the valley and says, "Woe is me," and they whine and complain and sometimes say, "God made me so that others could have something to wipe their feet on." The second type, what Bill calls the "good" Christian, runs through the valley "giving everything to God," denying they are hurting. The third type recognizes they are hurting and that there is a God who walks with them through the valley of suffering. Part of that process is lamenting, and another part is trusting. Recognizing that something hurts, really hurts, and that God still loves us and is with us isn't mutually exclusive.

I agree with Bill that the third type—simultaneously hurting and trusting—is the healthiest response. It's not easy to hold lament and murmuring in balance, and most of us find ourselves like Ping-Pong balls going back and forth between the two, but God is merciful and will see us through.

Remembering that afflictions on earth prepare us for honor in heaven can help us stay on track. Brooks wrote, "Consider, that the trials and troubles, the calamities and miseries, the crosses and losses that you meet with in this world, is all the hell that ever you shall have. Here you have your hell; hereafter you shall have your heaven. This is the worst of your condition, the best is to come."[22] For the Christian, this life is as bad as it's ever going to be. For the nonbeliever, this life is as good as it will ever be unless they repent.

Finally, discard the lie that discomfort means God has left you or is displeased with you. Learn that the process toward growth, maturity, and contentment with God can be a severe one. That's where spiritual freedom is found. I've leaned on Thomas Brooks so much for this chapter that it's fitting to let him close it:

When a Christian under great troubles, deep distresses, and most deadly dangers, prays more for the sanctification of affliction than the removal of affliction; when he prays more to get off his sins than to get off his chains; when he prays more to get good by the rod than to get free from the rod; when he prays more that his afflictions may be a refining fire than a consuming fire, and that his heart may be low and his graces high, and that all his troubles may wean him more from this world, and ripen him the more for the glory of that upper world—it is a great demonstration of the special presence of God with him in all his troubles and deep distresses.[23]

# 7

# DISMANTLING THE DEMAND FOR A SIN-FREE LIFE

*Learn the Lessons That Our Struggles*
*Against Sin Can Teach Us*

*I do not understand what I do. For what I want*
*to do I do not do, but what I hate I do.*

ROMANS 7:15

S ticky sin" describes moral issues that tend to stick around. We fall, and then we fall again. Or we finally get victory and then catapult into pride because of our victory. Or we use one sin (pride) to fight against another sin (gluttony) and realize we're just trading sins, not overcoming sin.

Of everything I had to unlearn, one of the biggest was my faulty understanding of temptation. I especially want younger Christians to know that to be human is to be tempted. Thomas Brooks wrote these insightful words:

> The eagle complains not of her wings, nor the peacock of her train of feathers, nor the nightingale of her voice—because these are natural to them. No more should saints [complain] of their temptations, because they are natural to them. Our whole life, says Augustine, is nothing but a temptation; the best men have been the worst tempted; therefore, remain silent before the Lord.[1]

If you think you can become so holy, disciplined, and consecrated that you leave temptation behind, you are in for a bitter disillusionment. Remember, even Jesus was tempted.

Your temptations will die when you die, but not one second before.

> Who can say, "I have kept my heart pure;
> I am clean and without sin"? (Proverbs 20:9)

> Indeed, there is no one on earth who is righteous,
> no one who does what is right and never sins.
> (Ecclesiastes 7:20)

Of course, one major difference between the temptations Jesus faced and our temptations is that we give in to them on occasion. If you face frequent temptation and sometimes failure, all it means is that you're alive. Welcome to the human race!

When we dive deeper into the art of unlearning, we can begin to see the good that comes from fighting temptation, and how even this struggle is a necessary and precious part of life in Christ. We need to unlearn the demand that our struggle against sin should cease, and learn the value of staying engaged in the battle against sin.

If we don't unlearn the demand for a sin-free or even temptation-free life, we will become discouraged when temptation and failure overtake us; our sense of intimacy with God will be hindered; and we will be imprisoned by our own self-righteousness. We will also become proud and blind. Temptation and sin are a part of our lives, whether we admit it or not. Therefore to be unaware of them, or to think of ourselves as immune from them, forces us into spiritual blindness and denial, which has myriad unfortunate consequences, beginning with a judgmental spirit.

Puritan John Owen provided extraordinary insights about sin. In his book on mortification, he called out a selfish desire to be free from sin primarily because we hate the consequences of that sin (a man may hate his temper because it cost him his marriage; a woman may hate her sloth because it cost her her job) rather than hating our sin because it is hateful to God.[2] What we really hate, then, isn't our sin as much as it is the misery it brings us.

When our hearts remain in this condition, God may allow a particular sin to remain to awaken us to our self-love: "You set yourself with all diligence and earnestness to mortify such a lust or sin; what is the reason of it? It disquiets you, it has taken away your peace, it fills your heart with sorrow and trouble and fear; you have no rest because of it."[3] But these are the wrong motivations.

Accordingly, what if God allows a sin to perplex us and disquiet us in order to awaken us to other sins we are ignoring that are just as displeasing to God? God can use the sin and temptation we have become aware of to fight sin we are not aware of (and perhaps have become comfortable with).

A seasoned counselor told me of his work with a middle-aged man who continued to struggle with the allure of porn on occasion. He'd have victory for a while, then fall back into it, feel great shame, and set up an appointment with the counselor to find out what went wrong. "He earnestly wants to obey Christ," the counselor told me, "and in every other area, he walks in obedience more than just about any man I work with. But every six months, maybe even longer, he'll give in to this temptation."

The counselor discovered that this man defined his holiness by how long it had been since he had looked at porn. If not for a long time, he concluded he was walking in God's favor; if recently, he lived with great shame.

"The root of this was a theological error," the counselor explained. "He is righteous in Christ. He is perfect in Christ. He is not righteous because he hasn't looked at porn in a long time. He is not out of God's favor because he has fallen again. God doesn't keep a calendar, determining whether to favor him or discipline him based on how long he has avoided porn, but he has a very difficult time letting that idea go. I wonder if God allows his temptation to remain to transform the way he looks at God, himself, holiness, and his own salvation. Despite his longtime Christian commitment and his earnestness in seeking God, I think he still lives in a works-righteousness mentality."

Here is where I must confront my own weaknesses as a pastor and thinker and admit I am still learning to dismantle the lies. If I had worked with that man, 90 percent of my focus would have been on curing him rather than on seeking a deeper theological understanding.

We all have our struggles, and it's not wrong to long for victory over any particular one. But we do need to let go of the notion that we can grow out of temptation or that our favor with God rests on a "sobriety date." I realize such dates may have a place in recovery, but they don't determine God's favor and blessing. Learn how to use temptation and even occasional failure as a pathway to greater intimacy with God, integrity for yourself, and connection with others.

## TEMPTATION'S TRIUMPHS

In his book *Precious Remedies Against Satan's Devices*, Thomas Brooks identified several benefits we can gain as we engage in our continual war against sinning.*

**1. Our struggles keep us humble.** Again and again, I am struck by the ancients' (more importantly, Scripture's) clarion call that our greatest enemy is pride. I'll cite a few Scripture verses here and will point to many more in the footnote, which I encourage you to read if you're not convinced about this:†

- "Whoever has haughty eyes and a proud heart, I will not tolerate" (Psalm 101:5).
- "I [wisdom] hate pride and arrogance" (Proverbs 8:13).
- "The LORD detests all the proud of heart. Be sure of this: They will not go unpunished" (Proverbs 16:5).
- "God opposes the proud but shows favor to the humble" (James 4:6).

---

* In this section, I'm summarizing part 3 of Brooks's teachings in his book *Precious Remedies Against Satan's Devices*, Grace Gems, accessed April 2, 2025, www.gracegems.org/Brooks/precious_remedies_against_satan7.htm. Here Brooks reflects on "Satan's devices to keep saints in a sad, doubting, questioning, and uncomfortable condition."

† Please take time to read these verses as well: Leviticus 26:19; Job 33:17; Psalm 101:5; Proverbs 8:13; 16:5; Isaiah 2:17; Ezekiel 7:24; Daniel 4:37; Zephaniah 3:11; Luke 1:51; Romans 12:16; James 4:6; 1 Peter 5:5.

The fact that we don't think pride is our biggest problem is the biggest symptom of pride. The first thing we must dismantle is denying that pride is our biggest problem. No matter what our sin struggle is, it has its root in pride. Our battles against sin can in some odd way lead to a greater absence of pride by keeping us humble. Of course, it would be monstrous to suggest that we should be lax about other sins so we don't fall into the greater sin of pride. Instead, let's learn that God can and does use one sin to treat another. He is so sovereign, powerful, and brilliant that he can make even our sins serve our freedom from sin.

**2. Our struggles with temptation make us continually dependent on God and his resources.** They regularly remind us that we don't possess all that we need to live life in Christ. There is no "Superman" or "Superwoman" in the Christian world; there is only a super Savior. Since we never rise above temptation, we never rise above our dependence on God. Life in Christ is never an independent life; it is always sustained by God's ever-present grace. We don't grow out of our need for God. Periodic defeat, though humiliating, is an effective reminder of our dependence on God. It's a sad fact of human nature, but the truth is, if we can do something without God, we probably will (or at least we'll try). If we don't sense our need for his help, we'll collapse into practical atheism.

**3. Our struggles against sin keep us mindful of the grace and kindness of Christ for the pardon he won on our behalf.** We remain sensitive to how much we need Christ's sacrifice, as horrible as it was, and how wonderful Jesus is to offer himself as he did when we were and are so desperate for what his sacrifice won. The more I fight for my freedom, the more I worship the Christ who died for my freedom. I go through seasons where I sense more defeat than victory, but this is when I appreciate these words from Robert Murray

M'Cheyne: "For every look at yourself, take ten looks at Christ."[4] With our eternal righteousness established in Christ, we can face the failure of our temporary human righteousness on earth. We're not fighting for our salvation, our acceptance, God's affirmation, or God's approval. We're fighting for our freedom, and Christ's victory on the cross and his promise of the Holy Spirit give us hope, courage, perseverance, and the grace to endure our wounds, rise from the dust, and stand to engage in the fight for freedom once again.

**4. Our struggles against sin help us avoid becoming too affectionate toward the world at large.** We realize that though this created world is good and filled with many celebrated and legitimate pleasures, it is still a fallen world with many encroaching dangers that humiliate and ruin us (and, when given into, inevitably disappoint us). Enjoy the world, but don't love the world. Our sin keeps us in a state of hunger for the life to come—ice cream without calories! Laughter without ridicule. Relationships without betrayal. Adrenaline without danger. It reminds us that this world in its present state is not our final home and that, as wonderful as life in Christ is now, it will be even better in the life to come.

**5. Our battles against sin make us heartsick now, as we wait to be fully present with the Lord one day.** Accepting sin as a reality does not mean giving in to sin more easily. Continuing to fight against sin has an enormously valuable spiritual benefit—it points us toward heaven. We grow weary and discouraged and long for the day when we don't hurt and aren't hurt. We marvel how, even though God has been so good to us and revealed the way to the abundant life, we are still so easily lured away toward lesser pleasures and selfish purposes and become quick to choose a lesser life. Or we get tired of mean and cruel people who momentarily prosper. Only when Christ is universally recognized as Lord, King, and Savior and we live in our resurrected bodies will we discover the fullness of the eternally abundant life. Obedience is based on acknowledging Christ as King and Lord. Disobedience is a futile attempt to dethrone him.

**6. Our struggles against sin give us compassion and empathy for others who fight temptation and occasionally fall into sin themselves.** We recognize weakness and sin as universal and circle back to the humble recognition that we are all desperate for the grace, empowerment, healing, and wholeness offered through Christ and his Spirit. There is only one hero in Scripture and the Christian faith, and that hero is not and never will be us. Brooks takes this so wonderfully far that he even urges believers to "repent for their being discouraged by their sins." Brooks wrote:

> [Their discouragement] springs from their ignorance of the richness, freeness, fullness, and everlastingness of God's love; and from their ignorance of the power, glory, sufficiency, and efficacy of the death and sufferings of the Lord Jesus Christ; and from their ignorance of the world, glory, fullness, largeness, and completeness of the righteousness of Jesus Christ; and from their ignorance of that real, close, spiritual, glorious, and inseparable union which exists between Christ and their precious souls.[5]

In this light, the struggle against sin is a small part of an overall abundant, rich, prosperous, and glorious life, wherein even the seemingly worst parts produce good things.

Though our personal struggles may change over the years, they won't cease. We must dismantle the temptation to make the Christian faith about us or our example; it is entirely about Jesus' sufficiency and righteousness.

The work I'm doing on dismantling the demand for a sin-free life is bringing about one of the biggest changes in my life in recent years. For decades, I wanted to impress people (I'm sorry; that's pathetic, I know). I wanted to be an example who could say what Paul said to the Corinthian believers: "Follow my example, as I follow the example of Christ" (1 Corinthians 11:1). I feared that owning up to my imperfections would impair my ministry and lead others astray until I realized the freedom that comes from reminding myself that if I had never lived or if I were to die tomorrow, God's work wouldn't have missed or won't miss a beat. God doesn't need me, and I can't bring his work down. One hundred percent of my focus should be on exalting Christ, seeking creative ways to invite others to be enamored by the beauty of Christ, and calling everyone to the joy of being found in Christ.

How I longed for God to complete his work and let me be a model of one who *always* walked faithfully in Christ. And how I worried that my pathetic weakness would tarnish what wisdom he had managed to entrust me with in spite of myself. But that fear is evidence itself of how self-absorbed I am, which may well be my greatest sin. Whether God's work is advanced through his victory in our lives or his testimony of how he uses weak, fallible people is his to determine.

I'm sure Abraham isn't proud that everyone can read about how he offered his wife to two different rulers, on two different occasions, merely to save himself (sticky sins indeed!). David doesn't welcome the millennia of readers who are aware of his adultery and murder; Peter isn't proud of his cowardice; Paul never stopped regretting his misplaced murderous zeal. Yet the church has been built on the backs of their failures, even as God may choose to bless the contemporary church with our failures.

In my blog (www.garythomasbooks.substack.com), I list a year-end recommendation of books I've read. One year, two of those books were written by people who eventually resigned their positions in ministry due to self-admitted failures. I wondered if I'd get criticized for including these books, but then I asked myself, *Should I pretend the books aren't helpful or powerful because they were written by people who didn't live up to their calling?*

I'm not going to stop reading David's psalms, and I can be inspired by the challenging words of imperfect men and women today. If the books point me to Jesus, help me rely on Jesus, and lead me to worship Jesus, they are serving their purpose, and I can all but put to the side the person who wrote them. What I had to learn is that canceling books feeds into celebrity culture because it can present a view of human existence that doesn't align with Scripture.

Cancel culture isn't just a stranger to grace; it is an enemy of grace that demonstrates a complete ignorance of the Bible's description of the universality of sin. If I believe a prominent person is unrepentant in their sin, I'm going to walk away from their ministry but with a much different attitude than that attitude of condemnation I used to have. As God leads, I will pray for them. In my own mind, I may see this season in their lives as a necessary prelude for God to finally pierce their spiritual blindness and perhaps lead them on to an even more fruitful ministry.*

A teacher or pastor being "above reproach" (1 Timothy 3:2) isn't a low bar, but James 3:2 ("we all stumble in many ways"), which speaks of leaders, means it's also not perfection. It's somewhere between heaven and hell. While surely certain actions become disqualifying for a long season, if not for life, we will crush our leaders and do great theological damage to our own understanding of the gospel if we depend on the sinlessness of our leaders rather than glory in the sinlessness and perfection of Christ.

---

* Let me stress that if a minister is preying on women or exploiting God's people for money, there's certainly a place for protecting and warning potential victims.

For my own part, thinking I had finally achieved the sinless state I was working so hard to obtain could have ruined me, largely because I'd be profoundly deceived to think I was even close to being sinless. Without abundant struggles against sin, we all risk trying to attract others to us, wanting others to admire us or model themselves after us, instead of living to see Christ, and Christ alone, worshiped and adored. So I must humbly keep putting myself out there in the midst of my impatience, my love for sugar, my weakness in letting criticism bother me, my lack of forgiveness, my pride—things that people can see and judge me for.

May we never forget our potential to be dangerous, aggressively proud, and ambitious, how easy it can be for us to point to *ourselves* as the place where Christ is found, even when we know that Christ himself is the only answer. Thomas Brooks put it this way:

> Temptation is a school wherein God teaches his people to see a greater evil in sin than ever, and a greater emptiness in the creature than ever, and a greater need of Christ and free grace than ever. This is a school wherein God will teach his people that all temptations are but his goldsmiths, by which he will try and refine, and make his people more bright and glorious.[6]

Truth over teachers! What's important is *what* is being said, not *who* is saying it. While this statement may sound a bit absurd, it's rooted in Jesus' words: "I am the way and the truth and the life" (John 14:6). When I seek the truth, I'm seeking Jesus, even if he is heard in imperfect, out-of-tune instruments.

So we need temptation, even as we hate and fear it and long for all sin to go away. Stop wishing that life had fewer temptations and learn instead how to find refuge in Christ, meditate on the beauty of Christ's grace and forgiveness, and grow in humble dependence on Christ. Become more aware of your temptations and learn to battle them more faithfully. I'm not suggesting we stop fighting sin but rather that we use our struggles against sin to exalt Christ instead of ourselves. It's the great reversal.

## THE SINS WE CARE ABOUT

As an introvert, I find getting up in front of groups draining. I'm also self-conscious about my appearance. My bald head can shine in the lights, and I'm not the trim marathon runner I used to be. I feel humiliated at times to know I'm going to get in front of all those people and be too busy trying to preach to hold in my gut.

But God uses my preaching. I know he does. And I don't want to let vanity or shame about my physical body prevent me from sharing beautiful spiritual truths. So I've had to learn, *Just get up there, Gary. It's not about how you look; it's about how Jesus saves.*

I don't *want* to be thinking about myself when I'm getting up to speak, but I'm a sinful man. Even when we learn that temptations are essential, we may resent being tempted the way we are. We'd rather choose which temptations we face, but the reality of our fallenness doesn't give us that option. Besides, as I've read the Christian classics, I've learned that the sins I care about and focus on the most may be the sins God cares about the least. If we get too hung up on how our culture views sins, we can miss out on a deeper understanding of sin's root. I can manage the sins that would get me fired from my vocation, so that's what I'll tend to focus on. Money, sex, and power are the big three that seem to bring Christian workers down. But Puritan Richard Baxter calls me to go deeper:

Bestow your first and chiefest labour to kill sin at the root: to cleanse the heart, which is the fountain. . . . Know which are the master-roots; and bend your greatest care and industry to mortify those: and they are especially these that follow; 1. Ignorance. 2. Unbelief. 3. Inconsiderateness. 4. Selfishness and pride. 5. Fleshliness, in pleasing a brutish appetite, lust or fantasy. 6. Senseless hardheartedness and sleepiness in sin.[7]

*Ignorance.* The first thing Baxter tells us to focus on is a spiritual dullness where we are completely unaware and make no effort to find out or consider God's desires and commands. This is a growing problem in the church today. God demands all—Jesus describes life in him as "taking up our cross." To never consider what God wants of us by studying his Word, waiting in prayer, seeking counsel, reading books, or listening to sermons shows we are not taking God's lordship seriously. The secular adage, "ignorance of the law is no excuse" is pertinent here.

*Unbelief.* The second chief sin is that of the unbeliever who is committing the most serious of sins—not acknowledging God at all—or the believer who doesn't trust in God or put their hope in him, and thus lives a practical atheism, even while professing belief. Remember this powerful dialogue in the Bible: "Then [the Jews] asked him, 'What must we do to do the works God requires?' Jesus answered, 'The work of God is this: to believe in the one he has sent'" (John 6:28–29).

*Inconsiderateness.* This third sin surprises me. How many Christians today would consider inconsiderateness a bigger sin than fleshly lusts (listed at number 5)? But consider how many passages of Scripture berate "anger, rage, malice, slander" (Colossians 3:8), urge us to be patient (1 Corinthians 13:4), and call us to "slander no one, to be peaceable and considerate, and always to be gentle toward everyone" (Titus 3:2). Christians online can be some of the most inconsiderate people on the planet, not even realizing (*ignorance*, number 1 on the list!) how offensive they are in their own self-righteous denunciation of others.

*Selfishness and pride.* These sins come in at number four, which also surprises me. Many classics disagreed with Baxter and put pride at number one. Selfishness is primarily the fruit of pride.

*Fleshliness, in pleasing a brutish appetite, lust or fantasy.* Only at number five do we reach the sensual sins of lust, drunkenness, gluttony, and the like that today's church is fixated on. We have a distorted view of sin and thus a distorted view of holiness. We define godliness by what we lack (sensual sin) rather than by what we display (compassion, kindness, graciousness, patience, gentleness, and humility).

*Senseless hardheartedness and sleepiness in sin.* These words describe believers whose consciences are callous and insensitive. They are so cold to God that they don't know how cold they are. They are complete strangers to compassion, rarely display kindness (and certainly not to anyone they don't love), and are impatient toward everyone. And the last thing you'd call them is gentle. They are in an unregenerate state, but they don't realize it because they are focusing on the sins of others.

Baxter's list was written more than 350 years ago. Reading it helps me realize how sinful I am today. We might be able to belittle the sins this century seems most concerned about (sensual sins), but when I'm reminded that inconsiderateness, spiritual drowsiness and insensitivity, pride and selfishness, and other attitudinal sins might be even worse ("root sins"), I realize I will never be done in my battle against sin. Any thought that I could be is itself a sin!

## CLOSER TO GOD, CLOSER TO TEMPTATION

While I once hoped I could become so holy that I would be free from temptations, I could not have been more mistaken. The journey toward greater intimacy with God and a deeper life in Christ goes *through* greater temptations. According to Thomas Brooks:

> God had but one Son without corruption, Heb. 2:17, 18, but he had none without temptation. Pirates make the fiercest assaults upon those vessels that are most richly laden; so doth Satan upon those souls that are most richly laden with the treasures of grace, with the riches of glory. Pirates let empty vessels pass and repass, without assaulting them; so doth Satan let souls that are empty of God, of Christ, of the Spirit, of grace, pass and repass without tempting or assaulting of them.[8]

It is only through temptation that we can experience the fullness of the Christian life. "In the school of temptation, God gives his children the greatest experience of his power supporting them, of his word comforting of them, of his mercy warming of them, of his wisdom counselling of them, of his faithfulness joying of them, and of his grace strengthening of them: 2 Cor. 12:9."[9]

Do you believe that your temptations can help you learn to love God more? They can!

Of course, what we fear about temptations is giving in. No saint bats a thousand against Satan's pitching. And we understandably hate that. But in this fallen world, we'd be even worse without temptation: "You are bad under temptations; but doubtless you would have been much worse had not God made temptation a [medicinal] diet-drink to you."[10] It's striking out against that curveball for the third time in a row that teaches us how to finally hit one. We are the patient who resents getting tired, only to discover that in seeking medical care for our tiredness, doctors discovered a potentially terminal but treatable disease. The tiredness saved us!

I used to fear falling away from God or falling out of grace when temptation was fierce. One of my most formative songs growing up was Keith Green's "I Don't Wanna Fall Away from You." That song is a pantheon to young, earnest, sincere faith. I've wept to that song. But the mature can sing a different song: "Grace is never more acted than when a Christian is most tempted."[11] We don't fall out of grace when we are tempted; that's impossible. We must learn to fall *into* grace, thinking more of Jesus' glory than our sad estate.

Accepting the necessity of temptations is essential—there is truly no substitute—for God to call you into any kind of ministry. There are many angry people eager to disqualify anyone God is using merely because that servant being attacked is proving Scripture's truth that "we all stumble in many ways" (James 3:2)—a verse, by the way, that speaks specifically about *teachers*. None of us can maintain a proper attitude toward sin unless we unlearn the thought that we are above sin and temptation.

We are of no pastoral use to anyone if we are not mindful of the reality of temptation and our capacity to give in to it. Temptation trains us to help those who are tempted: "None so fit and able to relieve tempted souls, to sympathise with tempted souls, to succour tempted souls, to counsel tempted souls, to pity tempted souls, to support tempted souls, to bear with tempted souls, and to comfort tempted souls, as those who have been in the school of temptation."[12]

I once talked to a former pastor who stepped out of the limelight when he knew he had issues in his life that needed to be addressed (in his case, he definitely needed to step away). I asked him, "When you look back, what kind of people would you have hired if you were planting a new church?" Without hesitation, he said, "I would hire addicts who are in active recovery."

He wouldn't seek out the most pristine pasts he could find; he'd look for those who are most aware, most vigilant, and most dependent on *daily grace*. He saw their past as making them even more fit for ministry rather than disqualifying them. An important note: This man is referring to people in *active recovery*, not people who were caught and never really repented, those who just wanted to get back into the spotlight without having to work on the spiritual rot that led to their fall.

Let me also offer a word of hope for you as you grow older: You can eventually experience victory over prior temptations—not all temptations at all times, but you can become stronger, wiser, more vigilant, and less susceptible to the lies and deceptions of any one particular sin. It may even become more common to have a temptation pop into your head and you almost laugh: *You again with that silly argument? Not a chance! Get thee behind me.*

Unfortunately, new temptations quickly emerge to take its place. Even so, it's kind of fun to laugh at a former temptation instead of simply being terrified by it. Just know it can take a while and many failures to get there.

## PRECIOUS JESUS

The more I hate my sin, the more I love Jesus. The weaker I feel in temptation, the more I worship Jesus' strength.

Temptation can lead to a much deeper and richer life of worship. When we enter temptation, we can remind ourselves of what Jesus has done for us to gain victory over them. Consider these marvelous words of Milton Vincent that can stick with us through thick and thin: "The gospel is the one great permanent circumstance in which I live and move."[13]

Regardless of anything else that happens in my life—any loss, any shame, or any gain—the "one great permanent circumstance in which I live and move," the historical events that define me, sustain me, protect me, and keep me from despair, are the life, death, resurrection, and ascension of Jesus Christ, which won my heavenly Father's favor and the Holy Spirit's empowerment. No earthly event or circumstance can remove that favor and empowerment.

Anything that makes me love Jesus more, be more grateful for Jesus, think about Jesus more, honor Jesus more, and depend on him more isn't something I should despise. It's one thing to know we're forgiven; it's another thing to live in our need for ongoing forgiveness. That's the life we are called to now.

Jesus.

Always Jesus.

And why would we ever want to give up anything that reminds us of him, points us to him, and leads us to worship him more earnestly?

Dismantle the demand to be free of temptation. Learn how to use temptation to love your Savior.

# 8

# DISMANTLING APATHY TOWARD THE CHURCH

## *Learn to Be a Suffering Servant for the Church*

*I rejoice in what I am suffering for you, and I fill up
in my flesh what is still lacking in regard to Christ's
afflictions, for the sake of his body, which is the church.*

COLOSSIANS 1:24

*I will very gladly spend for you everything I have and expend
myself as well. If I love you more, will you love me less?*

2 CORINTHIANS 12:15

In May 1942, Czechoslovak resistance soldiers parachuted into Prague for the purpose of assassinating German SS General Reinhard Heydrich, the main architect behind the "Final Solution"* and the Third Reich's third in command after Adolf Hitler and Heinrich Himmler. While I hesitate to use an assassination as an example in a Christian book, the evil that Heydrich unleashed rivaled any murderer in world history.

Czech resistance fighters wanted the world to know that though their country was occupied, many of its citizens were not silent and passive. As the Czech fighters prepared to depart for their mission, each man was given a cyanide tablet with the explanation, "Our assignment is to kill him; it isn't to get away safely." *Our assignment isn't to get away safely.* Getting the job done is more important than surviving.

The Nazis believed in collective responsibility and would seek to destroy not just the resistance fighters who carried out the actual assault but anyone who helped in any way. To be captured was to be tortured; to be tortured was to be vulnerable to betraying others. These men knew they could have to face death to save the lives of their compatriots.

Thus the cyanide tablets.

Though the two soldiers who succeeded in delivering the fatal blow (it took a few days for Heydrich to die of his wounds) got away, they were predictably hunted down. The last stand took place in a church, where they and their comrades were overwhelmed by superior firepower. All the fighters who sought refuge in the church died from enemy fire or by cyanide when it was clear they would not survive.

The heroism continued. Bishop Gorazd, who was in charge of the

---

* The "Final Solution" refers to the systematic murder of European Jews by the Nazis, aiming at their ultimate annihilation. The full title the Nazis gave it was "Final Solution to the Jewish Question" (*Endlösung der Judenfrage*).

cathedral, wrote letters to Nazi authorities, personally taking blame for hiding the resistance soldiers, hoping to stave off repercussions toward his flock. He was only partially successful, and he ended up paying a severe price—a firing squad. Gorazd was later declared a saint by the Eastern Orthodox Church.[1]

I hate war, though sometimes it's necessary. I don't mean to glorify war in any way. But I want to suggest this question: Do we think the spiritual battles we fight today are as serious and as worthy of sacrifice as the military battles fought by the Czechs against the Nazi forces in World War II? Will we fight for our faith as courageously as the Czechs fought for their freedom? We will not use guns and grenades, of course, but will we sacrifice comfort, time, and resources for our heavenly King as much as soldiers sacrificed for their country?

The apostle Paul lived as if he were at war (spiritually speaking).[*] He was a passionate man, willing to sacrifice all for a great and glorious purpose. He poured himself out on behalf of the church. Some today may push back against this, arguing that today's church is so awful that it's not worthy of our sacrifice. But before we accept this line of reasoning, we should read how Paul described the many egregious sins in the churches to which he wrote. In Paul's mind, an imperfect church *is* worth the ultimate sacrifice. In fact, a sinning church increased Paul's fervor to purify it rather than to run from it.

The church today is under assault. When the church is under assault, Jesus is under assault. Paul, because he loved Jesus so passionately, was willing to suffer for the church's survival and prosperity.

We must dismantle our independent pursuit of God and learn instead to give ourselves fully, enthusiastically, and sacrificially to God's body and Christ's bride, the church. It is the center of God's

---

* See 2 Corinthians 10:3; Ephesians 6:10–20; 1 Timothy 1:18; 2 Timothy 4:7.

plan: "His intent was that now, *through the church*, the manifold wisdom of God should be made known to the rulers and authorities in the heavenly realms, according to his eternal purpose that he accomplished in Christ Jesus our Lord" (Ephesians 3:10–11, emphasis added).

If we focus only on our own spirituality, we are missing the biggest work God is doing in the world today. We are minimizing our faith. We must dismantle that approach. The more I learned to pour myself out on behalf of the church, the more I began to understand God.

## DO YOU LOVE JESUS?

It is increasingly important to dismantle apathy toward the church because the church seems to be losing favor at an astonishing rate. It is often seen as irrelevant at best and harmful at worst.

I was once invited on an Alaskan fishing trip where—let's be honest—I clearly didn't belong. My invitation was an act of mercy. These were titans of business and, in one case, Hollywood. They graduated from impressive schools and money passed through their hands more abundantly than the spawning salmon swam up Alaska's Ketchikan Creek in August. These were gracious, intelligent, and thoughtful men, not the narcissistic stereotypes people like to make the one-percenters seem. But there was one guy who was clearly networking on his way up. He intuited who was who, which people could help him climb a little higher. After he linked up with a couple dozen people, he finally got around to me.

"So, Gary, what do you do for a living?"

When I told him, he looked astonished, as if I had said I skinned golden retriever puppies to make scarves. After a long, awkward silence, he finally muttered, "Wow. I don't even have a question to ask you."

In a world full of business and entertainment, why give your life to the church?

For starters, to love Jesus is to love his church. Moses said, "The LORD's portion is his people" (Deuteronomy 32:9). Jesus told Paul that to persecute the church was to persecute him (Acts 9:4–5). The spirit of this age tends to be hyperfocused on individual salvation, but once we surrender to Jesus' lordship, we act as if there are no more wars to be fought, except perhaps battles of personal piety. *Any battles for personal piety that I lose will be met with forgiveness,* we think, *so in the end they don't seem to matter all that much.* The consequence is that we have a church without any purpose beyond self-enhancement.

A church without a purpose is a church without passion.

But listen to the words of a passionate man from two thousand years ago: "I have become [the church's] servant by the commission God gave me" (Colossians 1:25). Paul added, "I want you to know how hard I am contending for you and for those at Laodicea, and for all who have not met me personally" (2:1).

*How hard he is contending . . .* even for those he has never met!

Paul's identity can partly be described in two sentences. It's not a complete description, but it summarizes an essential aspect of who he was and what he believed:

I serve the church.
I work hard for the church.

Though we are more than servants of the church, we must never be less than that. To be true followers of Jesus, we need to say with Paul, "I serve the church," and "I work hard for the church."

We must dismantle the apathy that comes from dwelling on the faults of the church instead of on its calling and service to our Lord.

The worse the church gets, the less we should run away from it and shun it and the more earnestly we should work on its behalf to reform it.

What is *your* identity? If someone looked at your schedule, the focus of your prayers, and how you spend your money, would you be called a servant of God's church and someone who works hard for God's church? Or would others see you as someone who enjoys gossiping about the shortcomings of the church? Is your faith mostly about you and your advancement and spiritual growth, or is it about serving the body of Christ?

## WHAT IS A CHURCH?

By God's grace, I'm guessing I've spoken in about five hundred churches, representing just about every major denomination, geographic location (all fifty states and a bunch of countries), and demographics. Very few are alike, but they are all called "church." Not every organization that calls itself a church is necessarily a church, however, so for the sake of clarification, let me offer a description. I don't pretend to be a biblical scholar, so this isn't the kind of definition you might get from a theology professor. I'm sharing my assumptions about *church* for the purposes of this chapter. *Church* is a fellowship of people who:

- regularly gather and are committed to each other as brothers and sisters in Christ, and who proclaim Jesus as their sovereign Lord and Savior. They come together for regular meetings and foster a sense of belonging and commitment.
- are committed to obey, listen to, and discuss the Word of God as revealed in the Old and New Testaments.
- have a connection to and agreement with the historical beliefs of

the Christian church in at least their broadest form as found in the Nicene and Apostles' Creeds—the Trinity, Jesus as the only path to salvation, and other core Christian beliefs.

- focus on the worship and proclamation of Jesus as Lord and Savior that invites all generations and all ethnicities, rich and poor alike, with Jesus as the only center of their fellowship.
- are allied with the scriptural directives regarding the sacraments of baptism and the Lord's Supper. There should also be an emphasis on missions (evangelism/outreach) and giving to the poor, since these are emphasized in Scripture.
- are devoted to discipleship and spiritual growth, in which believers are encouraged and equipped to grow in their faith, knowledge of Scripture, and Christlike character. This can include small group studies, mentorship programs, and opportunities for service and leadership development.*

The church's central theme is the worship of our creator God and our participation in his renewal of the world through the gift of his Son, which was followed by the sending of his Holy Spirit, who empowers us to carry on Christ's work. We gather with the intention of making disciples who are eager to obey the commands of Christ (Matthew 28:19–20).

## SAVING THE CHILDREN BY SAVING THE CHURCH

I've read the words of some and listened to the voices of others who, in an ill-considered effort to recruit young believers, all but set themselves

---

* My gratitude to Jason Clark, a subscriber to my Substack column, for adding this emphasis.

up as enemies of the organized church. Because they know that fallen figures in the church may turn young people away, their strategy is to join in the condemnation rather than the reformation of the church to demonstrate they're on the "right" side.

But better by far than joining in the battle against the church is to give our children a vision of being servants of the church. I'll never forget talking to a young woman who was clearly upset by something going on in the corporate church at the time. I don't even remember what the issue was, but I'm pretty sure a dozen more issues have cropped up since then. Instead of defending what was happening (I couldn't), I simply pleaded with her, "Then help us fix it." I didn't defend my generation; I defended her calling. I asked her to lead her generation to serve the church so that the wrong she saw would not be experienced by her grandchildren.

Every Christian parent wants their children to follow Jesus. One of the best ways to do that isn't to focus merely on onetime salvation but rather on the lifetime call of service that can begin at a very young age. Children aren't the church of the future; they are the church of today. Christian history is filled with stories of people in their teens who, instead of living for themselves and spending their time on frivolous things and silly pursuits, gave themselves over to sacrificially serve Christ and his church (Francis of Assisi and Perpetua are two famous examples). In Scripture, we know that David was a teen when he defeated Goliath. Samuel heard from God when he was a young boy. Josiah was a boy king—barely a teen—when God used him to launch a revival in Israel.

I regret many things about my middle, high school, and college years. When it came to personal piety, my failings in those seasons were legion. What I don't regret are the hours spent serving Jesus and seeking to build his church. When I was at Kalles Junior High,

God called me to start Kalles Kids for Christ. In high school, a group of friends and I started a prayer group. I chose my university almost solely because I wanted to serve in the college ministry group that existed at the time. (I'm not necessarily recommending that as a method of choosing where to study, but it proved to be right for me.)

I thought I was serving the church, but the church was in fact serving *me*, keeping me from wasting good years on selfish pursuits. Don't get me wrong, I wasted much time. But not nearly as much as I could have. If someone is old enough to be a Christian, they are old enough to be a servant of the church. If they are old enough to be "saved," they are old enough to serve. Our youth need the church even more than the church needs them.

With provocative language, Augustine compares the church to a ship amid the world's raging seas:

Now by this very journey we are exposed to waves and tempests, but we must needs be at least in the ship. For if there be perils in the ship, without the ship there is certain destruction. For whatever strength of arm he may have who swims in the open sea, yet in time he is carried away and sunk, mastered by the greatness of its waves. . . .

Meanwhile the ship which carries the disciples, that is, the Church, is tossed and shaken by the tempests of temptation; and the contrary wind, that is, the devil her adversary, rests not, and strives to hinder her from arriving at rest. . . . For though the ship still be in trouble, still it is the ship. She alone carrieth the disciples, and receiveth Christ. There is danger, it is true, in the sea; but without her there is instant perishing. Keep yourself therefore in the ship, and pray to God.[2]

We need to keep building the church because in doing so we are building our own lifeboat. Life inside the ship is far from perfect. In fact, the only place worse is life *outside* the ship in the raging seas.

## THE SUFFERING SERVANT

The story is told of the time the renowned evangelist D. L. Moody and Henry Varley, an English butcher and lay preacher, were leaving a prayer meeting when Varley said to Moody, "The world has yet to see what God will do with a man fully consecrated to him." According to one of Moody's biographers, Moody was so gripped by the quote that he vowed to become that kind of man.[3]

Varley's sentiment is honorable, but it leaves me scratching my head. I don't know how you can get much more "fully consecrated" than the apostle Paul, who famously said, "Now I rejoice in what I am suffering for you, and I fill up in my flesh what is still lacking in regard to Christ's afflictions, for the sake of his body, which is the church" (Colossians 1:24).

It's not as though Jesus' afflictions lack anything to win our salvation; it's that Jesus' afflictions aren't over in this sense: Jesus has such an intimate connection with the church that when the church suffers, he suffers. Jesus calls the church his bride. The most intimate of all human relationships is the metaphorical connection between Jesus and his church.

In another metaphor, the church is an extension of Christ's own body (1 Corinthians 12:21–31), which is why if the church suffers, Jesus suffers. When Saul persecuted the early church, Jesus asked him, "Why do you persecute *me*?" (Acts 9:4, emphasis added). If the church is Christ's bride and body, we can be certain of this: *When we work to build the church, we please Jesus in a special sort of way.*

And because the church is dynamic—growing, developing, ever being built up—it requires new sacrifice and new afflictions on its behalf. J. B. Lightfoot explains, "It is a simple matter of fact that the afflictions of every saint and martyr do supplement the afflictions of Christ. *The Church is built up by repeated acts of self-denial in successive individuals and successive generations.*"[4]

The church must be built; it is God's only plan. How will it be built? On the backs of faithful, suffering believers.

## SERVING MORE THAN SUFFERING

In my marriage seminars I have to be careful because I'll sometimes use stories of heroic love in the face of a spouse's death. Most of us think that if our spouse is facing a terminal illness, we'll step up. Most often, however, marriage calls us to *daily* service more than heroic suffering, and the same is true of the church.

Daily, mundane service for the church includes:

- the challenges of living with stumbling believers

    It can be frustrating and embarrassing to be associated with anti-intellectual people, hypocrites with very public falls whose apologies are almost as embarrassing as their sin, or narcissistic people who co-opt Bible studies and small groups with silly questions and comments. My love for the church isn't because it's lovable; often it's not. I love the church because I worship Jesus, and the church is his bride. While many church members inspire me with their devotion, teach me through their intellect, and humble me with their love, many others feel more like the embarrassing uncles and aunts at the family gathering who have a right to be there but probably wouldn't be invited otherwise.

- time and talents

The church needs Bible study teachers, church education teachers, deacons, elders, worship leaders, facilities helpers, etc. Who has time for that? Suffering servants make time. The facilities team at our church in Colorado is up at 4:30 a.m. on a snow day to make room for a thousand cars to find a place to park. The worship team shows up by 6:00 a.m. every Sunday of the year. The Manna team sets up an amazing store in the lobby (serving hundreds of needy families) every Monday, and it's gone by Wednesday. I get exhausted just thinking about it.

The question isn't, *Do I have the time?* The question is, *Am I called and will I make the time?*

- giving money

Giving should hurt, at least a little. If we don't wince a little bit at the end of the year when we do our taxes and investigate how much we've donated, we're probably not giving passionately, and certainly not sacrificially. We don't want to be the person who gives their spouse nothing more than a grocery store card and grocery store carnations on their twenty-fifth wedding anniversary. It sounds like, "I know I have to give you something, so here you go."

- praying for the church

God bless the Epaphrases of the church. Paul commended this man in his letter to the Colossians: "Epaphras, who is one of you and a servant of Christ Jesus, sends greetings. He is always wrestling in prayer for you, that you may stand firm in all the will of God, mature and fully assured" (4:12). Paul was also a frequent prayer servant for the church: "I thank my God every time I remember you. In all my prayers for all of you, I always pray with joy" (Philippians 1:3–4).

Do you pray for God to raise up young women and men to serve the church? Do you pray for the faithfulness of national ministries and those in your local church? Do you lift up other traditions of Christianity around the world, asking God to refine and bless them? Praying not only effects change, but it also affects our hearts, giving us greater passion for the work of Christ through his body.

I love being a guest preacher at Shoreline Community Church in Monterey, California. During every worship service, they pray out loud for another local congregation. This models exactly the right spirit, displaying the heart of Christ for his work through his entire body of believers, his beloved church.

- showing up on Sunday

It's not easy to get to church, especially if you have young children (or for Texans, a ranch house getaway in the Hill Country; for Coloradans, a ski chalet in the mountains; for Chicagoans, season tickets to the Bears). At the end of a long workweek and on the cusp of starting another one, it makes total sense if families say, "We're just too tired" or "We'll just watch online." But as a point of reference, the early church existed in a world where Sunday was the *first day* of the workweek. Why is that significant? To honor the resurrection, believers got up very early to celebrate *before starting their workday*. The church did not gather on a weekend. The equivalent today would be churches meeting on Monday morning from six to seven. It took a few centuries for Christians to get the day off to go to worship. That's the commitment on which the church was built, and that's the commitment it will take for it to continue to grow.

I've worked on the staff of several churches, and I believe church staffs have a responsibility to make the members' time worthwhile by providing engaging sermons and meaningful worship, fostering a strong sense of belonging and fellowship, and creating opportunities for everyone to serve rather than simply listen. But keep this in mind: Church attendance isn't primarily a statement about your judgment on the church staff's competence; it's a statement about your passion for worshiping the resurrected and ascended Jesus.

I know this may be misunderstood, but in a sense, a full parking lot can preach a sermon to all who pass by, especially those who would never step foot inside a church. It's a visual picture that if many people are spending time on Saturday evening or Sunday morning worshiping Jesus, they may want to consider him too.

## SUCKING THE MARROW OR GIVING A TRANSFUSION

Paul's sacrificial attitude toward the church calls us to a new attitude of what it means to be a Christian. It's not just about personal piety or being personally inspired; it's also about being part of a community that proclaims Jesus as the risen King.

Years ago, I spent a week speaking at a church in Hong Kong. The pastor told me that one of his greatest challenges was the mindset of many people when coming to Hong Kong: *Suck all the money I can out of that region and then go back home with my wealth.* They didn't come to Hong Kong with a heart for the region or for ministry. It was more of a mercenary attitude. It's profoundly difficult for a pastor to build a vision for reaching a region when so many people are intent on simply *using* it.

I've met some believers who have the same mercenary attitude toward the local church. They are full of ideas about what should or could be done, but if you ask them what *they* are doing to build up the church, the reality is that they prefer to just complain.

Do you seek to suck the marrow out of your local church, or do you have the attitude of donating your own marrow to further your church's well-being? Do we have the heart of a suffering servant who would admit, "I think another church could meet my needs or at least my desires better, but I sense God saying, *Yes, you could be a captain or even a general at another church. But right now I need you to help plug that gap in that church.*" Is there room in our faith for that?

"Plugging a gap" refers to a Civil War battle at Gettysburg where Union forces were about to be overrun. General Winfield Hancock knew he needed to plug a hole in the line until backup reinforcements arrived, so he sent dozens of men to a certain death, confronting an overwhelming number of Confederate troops, to give the Union army time to re-form and win its victory (which it eventually did). The soldiers marching forward knew they would never come back alive (none of them did). But they believed the cause was greater than their own lives.[5]

Make no mistake: Since Jesus is the Suffering Servant, we should expect to suffer as we carry on his work. The etymology of the name Israel ("he struggles with God") signals "a limping people." Its name emerged from its namesake, Jacob, who wrestled with God until the socket of his hip was touched and put out of joint (Genesis 32:22–32). "Limping people" is a pretty good moniker for the church. The book of Acts chronicles a bunch of beaten-up, murdered, persecuted saints, but the Christians' suffering only resulted in more and greater victories.

The apostle Paul shows us how to maintain a proper attitude about suffering: *He didn't look at suffering in the light of how much it might hurt him but in the light of how much it might benefit the church.* He willingly faced shipwrecks, beatings, incessant travels, prisons, and the ever-present threat of death. While at Caesarea, at the home of Philip the evangelist, a prophet named Agabus warned him that if he went to Jerusalem, he would be put in chains (Acts 21:10–14).

How did Paul respond? He went to Jerusalem. The church there needed him more than he needed his freedom.

> I serve the church.
> I work hard for the church.

I need this truth! I cherish Paul's attitude because it's so easy to absorb the mindset of American culture. I'm at an age where many of my friends and many people my age talk about retiring. Yet my plate is fuller than ever and my responsibilities have increased. I sometimes fight for one day off every week. Talking to men who speak of never going into an office again naturally leads me to ask myself, *What would it be like to go sit on a beach regularly? Why am I still so busy?*

What I'm about to say is not to condemn others or even question their faith. For me, knowing what I know now, I can't retire while the work of the church advances. There may come a time, perhaps sooner than I'd like to think, when the church has no interest in what I do or say, but even then, my call to pray for her welfare and give toward her mission will remain. For me, if the church doesn't retire, I can't retire.

My older brother retired from his business (Microsoft) but not from the church. He left a long-standing vocation to spend *more* time serving the church and that's the attitude I want to have. It's the attitude of an inspiring friend of mine, Sherry Harney.

# YOU CAN REST IN HEAVEN

Sherry Harney has raised three boys, served tirelessly in a variety of local churches, coauthored hundreds of Bible studies, authored some incredible books, and labored in prayer for believers around the world.[*]

She personifies everything I'm talking about as someone who is a servant of the church and who works hard for the church.

One of her birthdays fell on the night a small group from their church was scheduled to meet at their house. It didn't even occur to Sherry to cancel the small group. Instead, she was on her hands and knees, scrubbing the bathroom floor and toilet—the one the guests would use.

On her *birthday*.

Sherry is sensitive to God's voice, and she knows that she tends to overdo ministry sometimes. Was this one of those times?

"I wanted to check in with the Lord," she told me. "I don't want to get back to the point where I'm overdoing things."

So she prayed, "God, I'm tired. It's my birthday, and I'm scrubbing the toilet. I'm just checking in with you to make sure I'm not overdoing it."

There was a quiet whisper in her heart from the Spirit: *You will rest in heaven.*

As Sherry told me this, her husband and I looked at each other and sighed with the satisfaction that comes from knowing you've heard "a word." I know Sherry's husband looks after her well-being. He makes sure she has times of fun. He's aware of her tendency to overdo things, so he will speak up when he sees it. But there are times when we're called to sacrifice and serve the church. And we, like Sherry, can find relief when we remember that suffering for God's church has an end. There will be rest in heaven.

---

[*] All of Sherry's books are worth reading, but *Organic Prayer* (Zondervan, 2024) is one of my go-to books to help people learn how to pray.

To be sure, there's a place for heeding the advice, "Rest, take it easy, and don't forget your Sabbath." I don't want to challenge that. But I also want to highlight Sherry Harney's example that life is about more than rest. The followers of the Suffering Servant will at times themselves become suffering servants.

Can you and will you say this?

I serve the church.
I work hard for the church.

One of the most glorious lines we could ever hope to see on our tombstone would be, "Lover of God, Servant of the Church."

If we—like Paul—see life as a spiritual battle, would it be for us a realm in which Jesus leads just a tiny contingent of faithful saints against an overwhelming hoard of enemies? Will we join the battle, putting aside lesser concerns to focus on Jesus' primary concern—the advancement and refinement of his beloved bride, the church? When I pray, I sometimes try to remember that I'm praying to a God who is at war. You don't go up to a general about to launch an offensive or who needs soldiers for a defensive maneuver and say, "Hey, General, when is that new car I've been praying about going to be delivered? Or, "How 'bout we move up the timeline on my job promotion?"

Let's dismantle apathy for the church. If our faith revolves around us, we'll soon grow bored of such an insignificant and maybe even narcissistic life. Let's learn the necessity and glory of working tirelessly on behalf of the church. May we all say:

I serve the church.
I work hard for the church.

# 9

# DISMANTLING A MATERIALISTIC WORLDVIEW

*Learn to Worship a Supernatural God*

When I preached my first sermon at the Woodway campus of Second Baptist Church in Houston, Texas, I was a guest preacher. Coming from the state of Washington, I was a bit in awe, because Washington churches don't have buildings like the one I was about to preach in (*two* balconies!).

I was also introduced to my armed guard. That was a first for me.

I vividly remember sitting near the front of the sanctuary when, during the opening moments of worship, I thought I needed to use the men's room. I probably didn't, but I get nervous sometimes and think I do. In this impressive sanctuary, I didn't want to feel the urge halfway through my sermon and start shaking my leg like Elvis Presley in a concert.

I figured that if I got up while everybody was standing during a song, I could slip out unnoticed, only to find out, to my chagrin, that when you're a guest preacher at Second Baptist, the armed guard goes where you go. He escorted me out and stood just outside the men's room until I came back out.

There shouldn't be any shame associated with needing to use the men's room, but I was still very embarrassed. I manufacture shame like McDonald's cooks up french fries.

After the service, the armed guard escorted me to my car. When I pulled out of the parking lot, there was an almost humorous sense of loss. My armed guard was gone! I'd only had one for about .000001 percent of my life, but it was kind of nice while it lasted.

Years later, I visited Saddleback Church and spent some time after the service talking with Rick and Kay Warren backstage. Rick wasn't feeling well, and Kay eventually insisted he go home to rest up for the morning (it was a Saturday night) leaving just Kay, me, and my wife, Lisa, in the room—except for the armed guard. I saw him raise his eyebrows and then watched as Kay nodded—code for *I'm safe, so you can go home now*—and he turned and left.

It was kind of insulting and kind of funny because in Houston *I* was the one being protected—and, in fact, when I returned to preach at Saddleback, one of their armed guards was assigned to watch over me (who knows, he could have been the same guy)—but on this occasion, I was a potential threat.

That's the world of megachurches, a world, I fully realize, many people like to lampoon. But if in this instance you think this level of protection is too much, you've probably never read the mail or listened to the anonymous phone messages received by these churches.

All of that aside, let me ask this: What if all of us could have roving protection like the kind megachurches offer to preachers or the kind that bodyguards offer to CEOs, politicians, and celebrities?

If you are in Christ, you do. The Bible calls them angels: "Are not all angels ministering spirits sent to serve those who will inherit salvation?" (Hebrews 1:14).

I confess—it can feel embarrassing to talk about supernatural beings. The materialistic mindset of our culture tempts me to mock myself. But God's Word is so strong, my own experience tells me otherwise, and the testimony of many others I trust has convinced me that I must dismantle a materialistic mindset—that the only thing real is what I can touch and see—and embrace the supernatural elements of life in Christ. The God we serve is a supernatural God who uses supernatural means to accomplish his purposes and watch over his people.

## A BIG GUY

John Bisagno served as a beloved pastor in Houston for decades. One of the families in his church had a daughter who attended a small college in Texas. The library where she studied was close to a patch of woods containing a shortcut to the dorms. The school had warned students not to use that trail at night because it wasn't lit. "Please stay on the lighted sidewalks," they urged.

But one late evening, the daughter was tired and decided to risk it. Halfway through the woods, she seriously regretted her decision. Have you ever met a person who just *feels* evil, like evil is emanating from their very pores? The student passed someone just like this, and the man looked at her with a devilish sneer. The young woman's blood nearly froze in her veins. The creepy man kept leering at her, but he didn't lunge or move her way, so she quickened her pace, just waiting for him to pounce after she passed. But he didn't.

She made it to her dorm room unharmed, but it took a long time for her heartbeat to return to normal. She told her roommate what had happened and said, "I'm *never* doing that again."

The next morning, the school announced that a young woman had been assaulted in those very woods the night before. They asked for information from anyone who might have seen something. The woman went down to the police station to identify the man in a lineup. It was obvious. She hadn't been able to forget the man's face, and she pointed him out to the police officers.

While I'm not sure why she was allowed to speak to him, she was able to ask him one quick question: "I saw you last night, and I'm curious. Why didn't you attack *me?*"

The man sneered. "With that big guy walking next to you? No way."

The young woman almost fainted. There was no big guy.

Or was there?

To this day, the family is convinced that God sent his angel, visible to this would-be attacker, to protect her. I've heard several similar credible accounts, and I trust Pastor Bisagno's vetting in this instance. One of my friends, Mary Kay Smith, has reviewed every book I've written since *Sacred Pathways* (my second book) was published. Her father worked at an overseas mission hospital and needed to pay for something with ministry funds. The hospital gave him a blank check, as they didn't know what the cost would be. He and his wife walked through the city of Durban when a man came up to him and said, "I want to shake your hand."

"Why?"

"I've been following you for several blocks because I wanted to pick your pocket. But I couldn't get close. My hand was stopped by something every time I tried."

The would-be thief opened up his coat and revealed wads of money stuck in a belt.

Mary Kay's dad told him an angel had prevented the thief from robbing him and gave her dad the opportunity to witness to him.

A biblical worldview should incline us toward believing such stories. We need to dismantle a materialistic worldview and adopt a supernatural worldview in which God protects his people, even through the help of angels.

## WE HAVE AN ENEMY

I'll never forget the time I was invited to speak to some missionaries in Japan, after which I enjoyed a short season of ministry. I loved my time in Japan. It's a peaceful and beautiful country. About a week in, however, my hosts took me to an area around a Shinto shrine, which was surrounded by the kind of lovely woodland park that normally floods my soul with peace, joy, and worship. Tourists flock to this place, taking pictures of the gorgeous grounds and chatting excitedly. But as soon as I stepped onto the grounds, I felt an overwhelming spiritual sense that communicated, *You are not welcome here.*

I had never felt something like that before, and it caught me off guard because these kinds of grounds—beautiful trees, greenery all around, gently flowing creeks—provide an experience I feed off of spiritually. This kind of setting is one of my favorite places to pray. But not this place. As a Westerner, I tend not to think of spiritual entities exuding their influence on a geographical basis, but even through my

Western prejudice, I couldn't ignore this feeling. Something was here, and it wasn't a fan of me or Jesus.

Is it too far out there, too uncomfortable, to talk about malignant forces tied to a location? The book of Daniel talks about an angel who confessed he was delayed from coming to Daniel's aid by the "prince of the Persian kingdom"—*not* a flesh and blood prince (10:13). The angel's mission was to join forces with the archangel Michael to overcome a malignant force explicitly tied to a location. And then, for emphasis, the angel told Daniel in verse 20 that his next battle was going to be with a similar malignant force—"the prince of Greece."

Old Testament scholar Iain Duguid points out, "Nor should we suppose that since Persia and Greece are ancient history, these angels are now resting on their laurels. The satanic forces opposed to the church continue to use the powers and institutions of this world in their struggle against God's people."[1]

Paul talked about the rulers and authorities in the heavenly realms in Ephesians 6:12: "Our struggle is not against flesh and blood, but against the rulers, against the authorities, against the powers of this dark world and against the spiritual forces of evil in the heavenly realms." It's plural. Ruler*s*. Authorit*ies*. Power*s*. Force*s*. Paul pointed to their defeat at the hands of Jesus: "Having disarmed the powers and authorities, he made a public spectacle of them, triumphing over them by the cross" (Colossians 2:15).

While we don't want to pay demons more heed than they deserve—they have, after all, been disarmed and defeated by Jesus—completely ignoring them can play into their hands. Duguid again: "When we don't recognize the existence and reality of the devil and his schemes, then we don't see the need to be encumbered with the whole armor of God. He finds us unprepared and easily overcomes us."[2]

Can I be honest? Admitting to my non-Christian friends that I pay attention to "spiritual forces in the heavenly realms" can be a tad embarrassing. But a scholar like Ian Duguid gets it right:

> Be convinced of the reality of the devil and his very real power. Be aware of the heavenly dimension of the struggle. But remember too that you don't struggle alone. Michael and the other heavenly figure had been engaged in this conflict together on behalf of God's people since the first year of Darius (538 BC). . . . Day by day and year after year, there are powerful heavenly forces engaged on our side of the struggle as well as that of the enemy.[3]

If this is true, and the biblical witness is pretty clear, shouldn't we at least be aware of what is going on?* And shouldn't we become more familiar with who is on our side? Can we drop our Western blinders, dismantle an overly materialistic worldview, and gain a new understanding of the powerful spiritual forces that are on our side?

John Mark Comer makes a convincing case that denying the reality of active evil forces has led to the number one cause of people rejecting God—the philosophical problem of evil.[4] If we remove evil forces from the equation, evil becomes God's *problem* instead of God's *enemy*. Spiritual forces can't accomplish evil except through material people cooperating with them. Jesus has disarmed these authorities, but people rearm them when they cooperate with the spiritual beings' desire to inflame their hatred, violence, and lust and then carry out great evil.

Why is there evil in the world? Because people cooperate with evil instead of surrendering to the power of God's Holy Spirit to fill us with compassion, kindness, gentleness, patience, and love instead of anger, rage, malice slander, filthy language, and lying (see Colossians

---

* John Mark Comer discusses these powers in more detail in his book *God Has a Name*, in chapter 2.

3:1–17). Comer's explanation is the best I've read of how to answer the question, "If God is good, why is there still evil in the world?"

And since there is evil in the world and spiritual enemies that oppose us and want to enlist us in their nefarious aims, it is ever more crucial to know of our defenders and helpers—God's servants, the angels.

## THE BIBLICAL WITNESS

One of the reasons it feels embarrassing to speak of angels is that they have been misrepresented in art and lampooned beyond all biblical recognition, so that to say you believe in angels sounds like you believe in something patently silly, like the tooth fairy or the Easter bunny. But the best response to popular culture's mischaracterization of angels isn't a denial of what is real, but a more accurate representation to replace the false one.

It's even sadder that Christians tend to speak of demons more than angels. I hear people speaking about demons all the time. Angels? Not so much.

Emphasizing demons over angels runs counter to the biblical emphasis. The NIV Exhaustive Concordance reveals that the Bible mentions the word *demon(s)* or *demon-possession* eighty-two times—not an insignificant number of occurrences—so it's not inappropriate for believers to speak of demons on occasion.

By contrast, the Bible mentions angels more than three hundred times, about a four-to-one ratio. If the Bible mentions something three hundred times, we should probably pay attention to it. We need to dismantle an overly naturalistic worldview and learn the blessings and reality of worshiping a supernatural God who watches over us in supernatural ways.* That's why for most of this chapter, I'll talk about angels rather than their evil counterparts.

I started thinking about angels only when I was assigned to preach about them once. After reading several books about them, I was embarrassed by how long I had ignored their reality. It is impossible to read the Bible and not believe in angels. When we start looking for them, they're everywhere.

When Adam and Eve were thrown out of the Garden of Eden, who guarded the way to the tree of life? An angel.

Abraham was told he would be the father of a boy, even though he was more than eighty years old. Who told him? Three visitors—two of whom were angels and one of whom was the Lord himself (Genesis 18:1–15).

Lot and his family fled Sodom and Gomorrah just before it got destroyed. If you recall the story, you know that Lot was slow to respond until—that's right—*angels* grabbed his hand and the hands of his wife and daughters and led them out (Genesis 19:16).

The Egyptians were chasing down the Israelites, determined to bring them back into slavery. Israel needed time to escape, but how do you slow down hundreds of furiously charging chariots, horsemen, and troops? "Then the angel of God, who had been traveling in front of Israel's army, withdrew and went behind them" (Exodus 14:19).

Daniel was thrown into the lions' den. The next morning, when King Darius came to the den to check on Daniel's condition, he was still alive. How could that be? Daniel told the king, "My God sent his angel, and he shut the mouths of the lions" (Daniel 6:22).

---

* Out of the many books about angels that I've read, the most helpful is David Jeremiah's *Angels: Who They Are and How They Help . . . What the Bible Teaches* (Multnomah, 2006). You'll notice my dependence on this book, and if you want a more thorough treatment, I recommend starting with this one.

Elijah was exhausted and spent, running for his life to escape the wrathful vengeance of Jezebel. He went a day's journey into the wilderness, collapsed under a tree, and prayed that God would take his life. Who comforted him? Who provided food and protection? An angel of the Lord (1 Kings 19).

*But Gary*, you might be thinking, *that's the Old Testament, which had kind of a primitive worldview.*

Fine, let's look at the New Testament.

Zechariah, husband to Elizabeth, went into the inner temple and was met by an angel, who told him he would father the prophet we call John the Baptist (Luke 1:11–17).

A young woman named Mary was visited by an angel and told she would give birth to the Messiah. Her fiancé, Joseph, freaked out—his fiancée was pregnant! Better divorce her. Who convinced him not to? An angel (Matthew 1:18–25).

Jesus was born in Bethlehem. God wanted to let the world know, beginning with the shepherds, but here's the thing: To see the baby, the shepherds would have to leave their sheep. Do you think any human being could convince them to turn their backs on their livelihood and go look for a baby? Not a chance. But a powerful presentation of heavenly beings? That'll do it! Angels convinced the shepherds to put their vocation on hold and celebrate the arrival of the Messiah (Luke 2:8–15).

Threatened by Herod, the baby Jesus needed to leave Bethlehem, but Joseph and Mary weren't aware of that. There were no newspapers or cable news reports to tell this young couple about the king's fury and why he was so upset. So who told Joseph to escape with Jesus to another country? An angel (Matthew 2:13–15).

Jesus grew up and was tempted by Satan in the wilderness. Who comforted him afterward? Angels (Matthew 4:11).

On the day before his death on the cross, Jesus was in Gethsemane with his disciples. In need of comfort and assurance, he asked them to stand by him, pray with him, and support him through the events about to take place. Though he was about to pour out his life on their behalf, every one of the disciples was failing him. They all fell asleep. Our incarnate Lord still needed encouragement, which couldn't be found in the flesh. Who did God send? "An angel from heaven appeared to him and strengthened him" (Luke 22:43).

Jesus was crucified and then rose from the dead. No human was expecting this or could understand it, and yet someone needed to proclaim to the women at the tomb the good news that would strengthen his followers and launch the church. Who did God choose? Angels (Matthew 28:1–10; Luke 24:1–12; John 20:1–10).

At the beginning of the book of Acts, Jesus gathered with his disciples, told them to wait for the Holy Spirit, and ascended into a cloud, signifying a finality—he would no longer appear to them as he had periodically over the previous forty days. The disciples were looking up as he ascended, trying to figure out what had just happened. Who did God send to explain to them the significance of the ascension and the promise of Christ's return? Two angels (Acts 1:6–11).

The church began to grow. It was an exciting but also a perilous time. James son of Zebedee had already been murdered (Acts 12:1–2). Peter had been thrown into prison and was being guarded by sixteen soldiers (vv. 3–5). Things weren't looking good. If he was to be the rock on whom Jesus would build his church, what would happen to the church if he died prematurely?

He didn't. He escaped from prison. How? Peter came to this realization: "The Lord has sent his angel and rescued me" (Acts 12:11). *One* angel overcame a Roman guard of *sixteen* trained soldiers.

On his way to stand trial before Caesar, Paul was aboard a ship being battered to bits during a howling storm on the Mediterranean

Sea. Everyone was terrified and had given up all hope. These sailors knew the sea and saw that they were in peril, but Paul was supernaturally calm.

Why? He was visited by (can you guess?) an angel: "Last night an angel of the God to whom I belong and whom I serve stood beside me and said, 'Do not be afraid, Paul'" (Acts 27:23–24).

But maybe you're thinking, *All these occurrences took place with just prophets and apostles, right—the really important people of the Bible? Angels don't have any relevance for normal, everyday people, do they?*

"Do not forget to show hospitality to strangers, for by so doing some people have shown hospitality to angels without knowing it" (Hebrews 13:2).

The Bible doesn't treat angels as being rare or insignificant. They are central in all that God did and does, from the moment of creation to the launching of the church to the building of the church today. We must dismantle any embarrassment that might come from talking about angels and learn the assurance, peace, security, and support that comes from remembering what and who God has made available for us in this life.

## WHAT ANGELS ARE AND AREN'T

History and popular culture get angels wrong unlike almost anything else. I've heard stories about the gazillion pastors who tell their congregations that the devil doesn't actually have horns and a pitchfork, even though nobody really thinks he does. I don't hear the same corrections about our misunderstandings concerning angels. The church today is particularly careless in this regard.

Perhaps the biggest misconception of popular culture is the notion that angels are advanced, evolved, or glorified human beings (thank you, Jimmy Stewart and *It's a Wonderful Life*). They're not. Angels were never human, and humans never become angels. Angels are distinct creations of their own kind. Not only do humans not become angels, but in some way, at least some Christians will help judge angels (1 Corinthians 6:3).

What's more, angels are messengers and warriors. They are not described in pious terms, nor are they pictured in the Bible as feminine. I'm not saying women today can't be warriors; I'm just describing how the Bible depicts angels. The only two angels specifically named have masculine names (Michael and Gabriel). The misconception today is making *angelic* and *goodness* synonyms. *Angelic* and *fearsome* would be closer to the truth.

In the Bible, angels are soldiers, not delicate darlings or moral exemplars. They are fierce and powerful and strike fear into the hearts of everyone who encounters them. Paul pulls back the veil of heaven to tell us that the day will come "when the Lord Jesus is revealed from heaven in blazing fire *with his powerful angels*" (2 Thessalonians 1:7, emphasis added). Though there are occasions when angels hide their glory from us (Hebrews 13:2), when they are seen as who they are in their full glory, they are exceedingly frightening.

Another scriptural truth is that angels don't appear to age. There are no "little angels" who grow up and get their wings. Why does this matter? It's fascinating when you think about it: *The same angels that protected and served Elijah, Daniel, Jesus, and Peter could be the ones protecting you.*

These are mighty warriors. When appearing to people, angels in Scripture seem to have forms that somewhat resemble human bodies, but they definitely do not look like diapered Valentine's Day cherubs.

Angels are not omnipresent. They can be delayed (Daniel

10:12–14). This is what makes me leery of the notion of a "guardian angel." In Scripture, angels are sent to do a task or deliver a message, but they don't seem always to be there. Omnipresence is reserved for our God alone.

## WHAT YOU GET

Angels are, first and foremost, messengers sent to serve God. As part of their service to God, they serve God's servants. When you trust in God, you get armed protection.

> *If* you say, "The LORD is my refuge,"
>> and you make the Most High your dwelling,
> no harm will overtake you,
>> no disaster will come near your tent.
> For he will command his angels concerning you
>> to guard you in all your ways;
> they will lift you up in their hands,
>> so that you will not strike your foot against a
>> stone. (Psalm 91:9–12, emphasis added)

Notice I italicized the word *If.* Nothing in Scripture suggests that angelic protection is promised to nonbelievers. Angels serve us because they serve God. Their aim is to do God's will, not protect humans at random. That's why I believe that a guardian angel assigned to each person is the stuff of legend, not the teaching of Scripture: "Are not all angels ministering servants sent to serve *those who will inherit salvation?*" (Hebrews 1:14, emphasis added).

Allegiance to Christ opens us up to angelic privileges. Jesus warned people from despising or having contempt for one of his followers* because "their angels in heaven always see the face of my Father in heaven" (Matthew 18:10). Believer, you have an advocate that has access to the highest places. Revel in that. Rejoice in that. Johann Peter Lange captured this beautifully: "The fundamental idea is, that the highest angels of God in heaven represent the smallest subjects of His kingdom on earth."[5] Make a commitment to Jesus, and you get the privileges of his "little ones." This is just one of a million reasons to become a Christian. Who wants to live without this kind of assurance and assistance?

## WHY TALK ABOUT ANGELS?

Why does it matter if we hold to a materialistic worldview in which angels have no role? Does it make any difference?

Indeed it does.

Angels lift our eyes from a broken, threatening, dangerous, and chaotic world to a universe in which we know we are never alone. We serve a supernatural God who offers supernatural protection. When angels appear, the thing they most often say is, "Fear not!" They see what we don't see, as when Elisha prayed for his servant's eyes to be opened and he saw the hillside filled with "chariots of fire," angels ready to go to war on Elisha's behalf (2 Kings 6:17).

After many conferences and not a few sermons, people sometimes say to me, "I'm going to pray for you because Satan hates what you're doing." I am grateful for these prayers and don't want a single one of

---

* Jesus uses the phrase "little ones" in this verse, which in an earlier paragraph refers to children, but most commentators understand that Jesus is speaking inclusively of all his followers by verse 10.

them to be muffled. But I can also rest confidently in the fact that for every demon Satan sends my way, God has a dozen angels to protect me.

Fear keeps our eyes on the enemy; faith keeps our eyes on our Friend, the God of the universe, and his friends, the angels.

A widow did an early review of this book, and she told me, "I feel the desperate loneliness of a new widow living in a world aflame with anger." When she read the part in this chapter about divine protection, she wept. She came to the realization that she is *not* alone. Her husband may not be beside her physically, but when needed, God's angels will be with her spiritually.

A materialistic worldview keeps us focused on the threat; an angelic, supernatural worldview keeps us focused on our protection. Those who think often of demons play defense; those who think often of angels go on offense.

More than 250 times in the Bible, God is called *Yahweh Sabaoth* (translated as "Lord of hosts" in the ESV, "Lord Almighty" in the NIV). *Two hundred fifty times!* "Lord of hosts" can be translated as "commander of armies," making him the God of angel armies. Through his revealed word, God wants us to envision, again and again and again, that when we serve him and when we need him, he has the largest army ever amassed to fight on our behalf.

Shug Jordan coached the Auburn Tigers football team from 1951 to 1975 and won a national championship in 1957. Jordan once asked one of his former players to do some recruiting for him in the Miami area. The recruiter asked Jordan, "What kind of players are you looking for?"

Jordan replied, "There are guys that you knock them down and they stay down."

"We don't want them, do we, Coach?" asked the recruiter.

"No!"

"Then there are guys who you knock them down and they get up. You knock them down and they get up. You knock them down and they get up."

"We want them, don't we, Coach?"

"No, we don't want them either. Get the guy who's knocking all these people down. We want him."[6]

Knocking everybody else down is what an angel does. Winning victory after victory is what an angel army is created to do. That's the kind of player you can recruit to be on your team when you trust in Jesus—the guy who can knock everybody else down.

Too many Christians overestimate Satan's power. Satan is not an anti-God who is just like God, only evil. He is a created being who is limited in many ways. In fact, someone much less than God will defeat him. A *single* angel will be the ruin of Satan:

> And I saw an angel [*one*—not even an angel army!] coming down out of heaven, having the key to the Abyss and holding in his hand a great chain. He seized the dragon, that ancient serpent, who is the devil, or Satan, and bound him for a thousand years. He threw him into the Abyss, and locked and sealed it over him, to keep him from deceiving the nations anymore. (Revelation 20:1–3)

There will be a glorious, terrible, and momentous day in which God finally says, "Enough is enough!" The devil is done. Finished. Utterly defeated. His time is over. God looks toward one angel and says, "Now. Take him out."

And that one angel does. That same angel may well be watching over *you*.

## THE LAMB

At the age of thirty-four, Sheila Walsh was a successful recording artist and cohost of the *700 Club*, the most-watched Christian show of its kind at the time. Putting on a facade, she was speaking to millions of believers on the air but was not well, trying desperately to keep her life together.

Twelve hours after the broadcast, this model Christian woman made a courageous and wise choice when she checked herself into a psychiatric ward, fearing self-harm. Being on a suicide watch meant someone checked on her every fifteen minutes. Most of the time, she felt catatonic, sitting there with her head in her hands, not quite believing what was happening. How do you go from encouraging and blessing millions to being locked in a room by yourself, with nurses regularly checking in to make sure you aren't harming yourself? What would her viewers say? What would the enemies of Christ who look for every opportunity to ridicule faith say?

Doctors and nurses and attendants came in and out on schedule, but one man visited who appeared to have no medical role. He wasn't wearing hospital clothes, and he didn't check Sheila's vital signs.

Earlier in the book, I asked if you had ever come across someone who just felt evil? This man exuded the opposite. His very presence brought a calm, peaceful, and safe spirit. He stood in front of Sheila, lifted her head, and placed a plush, stuffed lamb in her hands.

He started to walk out but paused at the door and said, "Sheila, the Shepherd knows where to find you."

You could be a young woman walking through the woods alone. The Shepherd knows where to find you. You could be a thirty-something celebrity in a mental hospital; you can't get away from God's presence. The Shepherd knows where to find you. You could be a widow, facing a new life without your husband beside you. The Shepherd knows where to find you. You could be a young dad, feeling overwhelmed by your new responsibilities, or a young adult at a rehab center, perhaps having alienated every one of your family members and friends. The Shepherd knows where to find you.

An overwhelming peace came over Sheila, allowing her to finally fall asleep. She woke up hours later on the floor, wondering if she had just had a vivid dream. But then she looked over at the bed, and the stuffed lamb was still there. "What a ray of hope in the darkest night in your life," recalled Sheila. Through a man who Sheila believes to have been an angel, God brought her healing.[7]

God was telling his daughter that there is nowhere you can go that my armies aren't watching over you or can't get through to you.

Christian, the Shepherd knows where to find you. Whether you are in a psychiatric ward, a prison, or the closet as your parents are in the middle of a fight, the Shepherd knows where to find you.

> If you say, 'The LORD is my refuge,'
>     and you make the Most High your dwelling . . .
> he will command his angels concerning you
>     to guard you in all your ways. (Psalm 91:9, 11)

Dismantle the impoverished materialistic worldview that says we are on our own, that our faith is just about human will, human understanding, human machinations. Learn the powerful biblical truth that there is an unseen world all around us, with real spiritual beings that comfort us, protect us, and serve us—whether we recognize them or not. When we align with Christ, these good and powerful forces watch over us.

# 10

# DISMANTLING THE ALLURE OF EARTHLY SPLENDOR

## *Learn the Rich-Toward-God Life*

*Do not work for food that spoils, but for food that endures
to eternal life, which the Son of Man will give you.*

JOHN 6:27

*If I glorify myself, my glory means nothing.*

JOHN 8:54

Years ago, some dear friends took Lisa and me on a canal cruise through the Burgundy area of France. Our friends are foodies in the restaurant business, so they were particularly excited about visiting a vineyard where the grapes for the most expensive wine in the world, Romanée-Conti, are grown.

For context, I know as much about wine as I do quantum physics, which is to say, nothing. So the romance of the moment may have been lost by the skepticism of my mind.

We drove up to the rows where Romanée-Conti grapes are cultivated. There was a dirt road, maybe eight feet wide at most, dividing the rows where the grapes for Richebourg wines are grown from the rows of Romanée-Conti grapes.

Romanée-Conti is such an exclusive wine that some vendors require you to first purchase a case (twelve bottles) of Richebourg wine. Romanée-Conti can set you back eight thousand euros a bottle, though some have been sold at auction for more than $20,000 a bottle. Richebourg seems like a bargain in comparison, typically going for around one to two thousand euros a bottle. In some cases, you must spend around $15,000 to "get" to spend another $10,000 for that one precious bottle of Romanée-Conti wine.

While our guide was talking, my skepticism about the price disparity between the two wines skyrocketed as I noticed how close the Richebourg fields are to the Romanée-Conti fields. "You mean to tell me," I asked the guide, "that the grapes right *here*" (pointing to the Romanée-Conti row) "are eight to ten times better than the grapes that are *there*?" (pointing eight feet away to the next row).

"Well," he admitted, "the grapes on that end vine there may not be all that different from the grapes on the first Richebourg vine, but remember, they're cultivated from the entire field and mixed together, and there really is a difference between the middle of the fields."

I've driven through vast swaths of Texas and Montana and have seen fields of corn that could have accommodated a *hundred* fields of

Romanée-Conti grapes. The vineyard we were standing in wasn't *that* big, making me think the difference couldn't have been *that* huge—not eight times better, anyway.

But those distinctions are defended with zeal. We met a woman whose family owned two rows of Le Musigny vineyard (also in Burgundy). Vineyard ownerships are mostly divided by rows, or even partial rows. Musigny produces a highly coveted grand cru wine, so this woman's family was offered four million euros for *two rows* of the vineyard. Two rows will cultivate enough grapes to produce about two barrels of wine a year. There is no way that amount of wine would generate more than four million euros during the family's lifetime, but owning part of a prestigious vineyard isn't always, or even mostly, about the money.

"It's a family thing," she said, explaining why the offer was refused.

This kind of phenomenon fascinates me, which is why when we returned from our trip, I did some research and found a study that explains why our brains think expensive wine is better than cheap wine (even if it's the same wine).[1] Knowledge of the price literally impacts our brain's processing of the experience. People most often judged what was marked to be the most expensive wine to be the best wine, which makes sense to me. If I had convinced myself to pay eight thousand euros for a single bottle of wine, I'd want it to be the best wine I've ever tasted too.

If you're a true wine aficionado, you may have already lost all respect for me at this point (which would be fair), but that experience led me to ask the question, Are the "finer things in life" *actually* finer?

Or do we just think they are?

I have no doubt that to a trained palate, a glass of Romanée-Conti wine is a significantly different experience than that of sipping from boxed wine purchased at Costco, but think about the study I just referenced: If you were to take a bunch of normal people who aren't wine aficionados and told them the boxed wine was more expensive than the Romanée-Conti, they might even prefer the boxed wine over the world's most expensive wine.

In fact, "counterfeit wines" are becoming something luxury wine growers must guard against. In 2023, *Town and Country* magazine reported, "Domaine de la Romanée-Conti implemented a variety of measures to ensure that history [namely, luxury wines being counterfeited] would not repeat itself: serial numbers on the bottles, hidden codes visible only by blacklight, tracking information embedded in corks."[2] The World Health Organization isn't convinced, releasing a report that 25 percent of all alcohol sold globally is illicit.[3] Note that it's not just the taste of the wine that exposes the counterfeiting; it's the hidden codes and tracking information embedded in the corks.

If you can counterfeit fine wine—convince people that a cheaper wine is the same as an ultra-expensive wine—is it really all that different?

So it's a fair question: Are all the "finer things in life" really that much finer? Or do we just think they are?

In the same way, are we seeking things in life that are drastically and dramatically inferior in the light of eternity? It's difficult to overstate this, as I do believe this chapter is a matter of life and death—life in the sense of abundant life, and death in the sense of spiritual death. If we get this wrong, we get everything wrong. It will impact how we spend our time, money, and energy, and it will dominate our life goals.

Until I looked past the allure of the world's splendor, with all its showy pomp and circumstance, I couldn't desire, much less strive, to live an eternally significant life. The world puts on a good show (that's what "pomp and circumstance" is all about). It can be gripping in its distractions. But like an expert magician who distracts us with clever sleight of hand, so the spirit of this age keeps us focused on what it wants us to focus on, distracting us from the truth of God's glory, goodness, beauty, and grace. It is profoundly difficult to refrain from valuing the things that appeal to our senses over the things that appeal to our spirits. The world clearly believes and lives by the assumption that earthly splendor is more delicious than godliness and living in the favor of God.

But is it?

## AN ANCIENT FRIEND POINTS THE WAY

I took another trip with a good friend, but this is one friend I've never actually met, though I have spent many mornings with him. His name is William Law (you've heard me mention him several times already). Law, who lived in the eighteenth century, wrote the magisterial Christian classic *A Serious Call to a Devout and Holy Life*, which celebrated the beauty and wisdom of all-out, hold-nothing-back devotion to God. His book evoked an image I couldn't get out of my mind for days, the kind of image that can reshape your life, reset your priorities, and then keep you on course. It has to do with basing one's life on knowing the *real value* of things.

Law's idea that captured my imagination is this: Someone who chases after the enticements and goals of the world—fame, affluence, reputation, power—and neglects the things of God is like a foolish person who chooses a *fancy coat* over a *vast estate*. The coat has a certain immediate value and appeal, but it will go out of fashion and eventually wear out. The estate endures beyond a lifetime and can produce enough income to buy a hundred fancy coats a year. But the foolish person, focused on immediate pleasure, comfort, and misguided priorities, grabs the coat and walks away from the estate.[4]

Then I saw how many fancy coats I chase. Caring what others think about me or say about me—that's a fancy coat. The vast estate is being passionate about and investing my time in helping others think better thoughts about Jesus. Focusing on the appearance or, to some degree, even the comfort of my earthly home as opposed to thinking often and longingly over the blessing of my eternal home—that's choosing a fancy coat over a vast estate. Trying to impress people instead of love people, preferring entertainment over service, choosing food and drink over the wellness of my soul, achieving my "retirement number" over heavenly riches—for so much of my life (a shameful amount) I was chasing fancy coats and didn't even realize it.

This was my call to unlearn the allure of a life with worldly satisfactions and learn instead the value of a life that is rich toward God—the joys that follow living a life based on Christ's commands and priorities. I want to cultivate a discerning mind and zealous heart that can look past the fancy coats and inherit a vast estate.

How about you?

At the end of the day, do you care more about how others affirm and respect you or whether God is pleased with you?

Do you care more about your earthly status than your heavenly destiny?

Do you seek to be comfortable in this world or rich toward God?

Mark Batterson puts it this way: "If you're willing to be demoted in the eyes of man, then you're ready to be promoted by God himself."[5] If you're unwilling to be demoted in the eyes of other people, you're disqualified from being promoted by God. The two aims are exclusive. It's the fancy coat *or* the vast estate, not both.

## RICH TOWARD GOD

I mentioned my fishing trip in Alaska earlier in the book. I must confess that one of my goals on the trip was to avoid embarrassing my son. He belongs in that crowd—he has two master's degrees from

Harvard and has a beyond-impressive job, but he has found a way to incorporate his passion for the poor into a stellar business success. I couldn't be more proud of him.

Yet during a dinner, with my son sitting right next to me, I was finally asked, "So, Gary, where did you go to school?"

I laughed. "Western Washington University."

There was an awkward silence.

"What's that?"

"A state school in Washington State."

No one has ever asked, "What's Harvard?" Or "What's Stanford?"

But my beloved WWU isn't exactly a household name. I found it on a list of top-ranking liberal arts schools in the nation, and I think it was ranked somewhere around 374, so when Graham got into Harvard, I wrote to him, "Congratulations on keeping the family legacy alive and getting into a top 400 school."

Listen, I value education. I would have loved to go to a more prestigious and rigorous school. But that's still a fancy coat. The vast estate is what we *become* through our education, not where we got our education.

Jesus once talked about a rich fool who, following a fruitful harvest, decided to build a bigger barn and settle down into a soft bed of luxury, selfishness, and leisure. "Eat, drink and be merry," the man said to himself, not realizing that his life of self-absorption would end *that very night* (Luke 12:19). This is the fate, Jesus observed, of anyone who "stores up things for themselves *but is not rich toward God*" (Luke 12:21, emphasis mine).

The rich-toward-God life is the most abundant life a person could ever choose, but shockingly it's not a popular life or even, in some circles, a respected life. In fact, it's more likely to be ridiculed. Others may even call it a life of poverty, but true abundance begins by adopting God's dictionary and God's definitions.

The good news is that the life that is rich toward God is a life we can choose to begin living today, regardless of age, income, vocational track, education (or lack of it), or marital status. We don't need anything but a new focus to grab hold of it. Seeing through the allure of earthly splendor and learning about this new life redirects how we think about everything—money, fame, relationships, time, recreation, energy, and focus. It transforms what we value, what we pursue, what we ignore, and what we pay attention to. It is, I believe, the best life we could live—the life we were reborn to live.

Sociological studies back this up. Harvard professor Arthur Brooks cites a University of Rochester study that examined the difference between graduates who had primarily "intrinsic" goals and "extrinsic" goals.[6] Brooks writes, "Intrinsic goals centered around fulfillment from deep, enduring relationships. Extrinsic goals centered on earning a lot of money, owning a lot of stuff, gaining power, or achieving reputation and fame."[7]

After a year, most graduates were pretty much on track to getting what they wanted, but those with intrinsic (relational) goals were happier. Brooks concludes, "If your life goals revolve around lots of money, prestige, and other worldly things, you are setting yourself up to have exploding wants and low life satisfaction."[8]

"Exploding wants and low life satisfaction" is the most honest yet brutal description of life in the West today. This is our invitation to learn the real value of things, embracing a life that is rich toward God—the ultimate and most important relationship of all. I'm not suggesting it's a life where we can't enjoy fine wine, good music, and what many call "the finer things in life." God created many of those things, and we can receive them with thanksgiving, joy, and even worship.*

---

* See my book *Pure Pleasure: Why Do Christians Feel So Bad About Feeling So Good?* (Zondervan, 2009).

But pursuing life in Christ forces us to reconsider what we truly value and pursue above all else. Frederick Faber wrote, "No one need be poor, because, if he chooses, he can have Jesus for his own property and possession. . . . We can exaggerate about many things; but we can never exaggerate . . . the compassionate abundance of the love of Jesus to us."[9]

I loved the house we lived in in Houston for our last six years there. The craftsmanship fed my soul as a writer and teacher. But when it became apparent that for the sake of the kingdom, it might be advantageous to leave Houston and go to Colorado (where we bought a house built in the 1970s with low ceilings and literally the ugliest master bathroom I have ever seen), I couldn't let that beautiful house in Houston determine our course. It's one thing to use things; it's another to be imprisoned by them. We couldn't get to Colorado if we didn't leave Texas.

We can't live obedient, God-ordered lives if our hearts are torn apart by competing pursuits. We can't "sort of" value what the world values and still "kind of" value what God values. The two ends work against each other, dulling our passion for one or the other. Jesus said, "How can you believe since you accept glory from one another but do not seek the glory that comes from the only God?" (John 5:44). The pursuit of earthly glory *keeps* us from seeking the glory that comes from God. We must cease the pursuit of earthly glory so that we even *want* to pursue the glory that comes from God.

If I "kind of" care what others think of me, I'm losing touch for that split second with valuing the presence and favor of God. When I live in a house, I try to think of it as a hotel room—some are nice and some aren't, but in the end it's not of ultimate importance because in due course I'm going to be checking out sooner rather than later. There's nothing wrong with enjoying a "hotel room" while you're there.

Appreciate it, thank God for it, and let it serve you in the moment. As soon as you insist on staying in it, however, you'll begin missing the very reason you traveled to a new locale.

## EARTHLY SPLENDOR

The story of Paul's appearance before Agrippa and Bernice is a prophetic warning for those who put earthly splendor (a fancy coat) over a vast estate (being rich toward God):

> The next day Agrippa and Bernice came with great pomp and entered the audience room with the high-ranking military officers and the prominent men of the city. At the command of Festus, Paul was brought in. Festus said: "King Agrippa, and all who are present with us, you see this man! The whole Jewish community has petitioned me about him in Jerusalem and here in Caesarea, shouting that he ought not to live any longer." (Acts 25:23–24)

Picture in your mind the illustrious and flamboyant Agrippa and Bernice entering an ostentatious hall. Everyone is flattering them, trying to get their attention and curry their favor. Many would like to *be* them. They stay in the best accommodations and eat the best food. They have servants and the power to kill men and women or set them free.

Bernice, by the way, was Agrippa's *sister*, not his wife.

But she lived with him.

Yes, there were rumors.

Now picture a poor bald prisoner with bad eyes, no bank account, and little earthly power, except for some status as a Roman citizen. He was single and alone, and his face showed the marked effects of many tough travels in a difficult world. He had been severely beaten many times and was once even left for dead. His back was a monstrosity of scarred wounds.

A lot of people thought this prisoner was toxic and deserved to die, that the world would be better off without him, which in my opinion is about the stupidest opinion in the pantheon of worst opinions ever. The world would be better off without Paul and his writings? I wish he had written twice the amount he did. What I wouldn't pay for a weeklong seminar with him, discussing things I need to know and apply in today's world. Yet these learned men, Jewish religious leaders charged with instructing and teaching the prisoner's people, wanted him to stop writing and speaking altogether.

When it came to status, riches, power, and influence, it looked like Agrippa and Bernice had won the game. Agrippa continued to rule for decades, and his allegiance to Rome would win him much favor and riches. Paul had just months left to live, and he must have looked (and smelled) pathetic in comparison. "You see this man—he is not fit to live!"

Agrippa and the religious leaders saw Paul and made a judgment about his worth two thousand years ago. We "see" Paul and his relevance and impact today.

Who really "won"?

Today, not a minute goes by when someone in the world isn't reading, reciting, or memorizing words written by Paul. That's not hyperbole; that's fact. Paul is never *not* being read somewhere. Forests have been consumed to produce books written about Paul's writings and thoughts. In the next life, I will gladly stand in line to get a cup of coffee with this man (though I hope chai tea makes its way into the new earth as well).

Get this: Bernice and Agrippa wouldn't even be remembered today except for their interaction with Paul. Their bodies have long since rotted, along with their clothes. The ostentatious buildings they enjoyed as their possessions are piles of rubble. If someone said, "Agrippa believed such and such," most people would say, "Who's Agrippa?" This couple's power was like a Texas rainstorm—you can't miss it while it lasts, but it evaporates as soon as the Lone Star State's sun comes out.

In fact, it was *only* their interaction with the "poor" Paul, the man who was not fit to live, that makes them even remotely remembered today. They didn't know that then, of course, and consequently looked foolish. Agrippa got everything wrong. He told Paul, "You have permission to speak for yourself" (Acts 26:1). He gave Paul *permission* to speak—as if it were his right to determine who could hear Paul. The religious leaders who wanted to silence Paul failed—big-time. We don't know a single one of their names. But today, when a Christian teacher mentions the name Paul, everyone knows exactly who they are talking about. Mention Agrippa, and you'll have to launch into a long backstory.

Take time to ponder this contrast, because history has few like it—immense worldly success interacting with wild worldly ignominy. Earthly splendor lasts no longer than the morning dew. Being rich toward God is an investment that grows through the centuries rather than being depleted in mere decades.

## THE HEAVENLY CITY VERSUS BABYLON

Next to the words of Jesus, the apostle John's book of Revelation paints the starkest example of being rich toward God in contrast to valuing the world. One of the main themes of Revelation is the contrast between earthly glory going down in flames and heavenly glory shining into eternity.

Professor of biblical studies Rodney Reeves writes, "The death of Christ exposes the counterfeit ways of the devil—his temporary power, empty riches, false wisdom, fleeting might, contrived honor, vainglory, and fake blessing. The slain-but-still-standing Lamb of God, on the other hand, is the incarnation of *true* power, riches, wisdom, might, honor, glory, and blessing."[10] The devil's attempt to overturn God is in macro what will be revealed in micro whenever anyone attempts the same. Reeves writes, "The next time you see someone trying to grab all the power they can get, manipulating people to their advantage, know that one day they will lose it all—just like the devil."[11]

It's comforting and spiritually helpful to remind ourselves of this. t's also vital to remember this, if we want to unlearn the allure of a life that is rich toward the world and instead value a life that is rich toward God: "Many see rewards in this life as the only things worth living for. We see rewards in the next life as the only thing worth dying for."[12]

I'm ashamed to admit that Revelation has never been one of my favorite books. It seems more bizarre than practical, but Reeves's explanation opened its powerful truth to me in his book *Spirituality According to John*: "To spend the strength of your days for the things of this world and then die in vain is such a waste. To give our life for the Lamb who overcomes the world so that we might live in the kingdom forever is true strength. The dragon loses; the Lamb wins."[13]

If you're looking for a succinct phrase to summarize seeking the rich-toward-God life, you'd be hard-pressed to find a pithier, more powerful line than "the dragon loses; the Lamb wins."

When evil seems to be soaring and good people are publicly shamed, say to yourself, *The dragon loses; the Lamb wins.*

When you're treated unfairly or laughed at for your passionate defense of the gospel, remind yourself, *The dragon loses; the Lamb wins.*

When your lack of earnings is ridiculed and your good deeds go unnoticed, cling to the truth that *the dragon loses; the Lamb wins.*

When even loved ones accuse you of wasting your life by seeking first God's kingdom instead of your own, say to yourself, *The dragon loses; the Lamb wins.*

To learn the rich-toward-God life, forget what used to impress you. What is wealth? What is power? What is influence? Who cares what citizens of the earth say about you when you are empowered by and celebrated in heaven?

God's love is better than worldly honor. God's eternal rewards are vastly more valuable than earthly accumulations. The favor of God is worth more than historical acclaim. The rich-toward-God life is about learning to place the same value on things and actions as God does, seeking to be rich toward God instead of rich toward and celebrated by the world.

*After all, the dragon loses and the Lamb wins.*

# 11

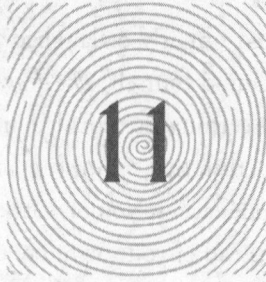

# DISMANTLING A SENSE OF ENTITLEMENT

*Learn What It Means to Be Rescued*

*In your distress you called and I rescued you.*

PSALM 81:7

The great Russian novelist Fyodor Dostoevsky was sentenced to death by the Russian government in 1849 for anti-government activities and taken before a firing squad. Imagine the terror while he stood there with fellow members of the Petrashevsky Circle,* chained and waiting to be shot. The moment of his death seemed inevitable.

Then he heard the order given for the soldiers to raise their guns. He could see the barrel through which the bullet that would take his

---

* A group of intellectuals who championed ideas considered to be subversive by the Russian government.

life was about to explode. And then, while Dostoevsky and his comrades were bracing themselves for the shots to be fired— rifles drawn in front of them less than fifty yards away—another order was given, and the executioners put their guns down.

Wait, *what*?

Dostoevsky later found out that government authorities decided to give him and his friends a reprieve, hoping for their gratitude and support. They were sentenced to four years of hard labor at a Siberian labor camp.[1]

A Siberian labor camp, especially in the winter, is no picnic. Four years living in squalid conditions without getting a single day off is a serious punishment. It would be natural to grumble more and more with every passing day. But given the circumstances, having been one finger twitch away from death, being sentenced to hard labor felt like a *gift* to Dostoevsky.

Dostoevsky never forgot this moment. He later used it to describe the feelings of a character in his novel *The Idiot*. If you thought you were about to die and yet got to live, and then you created some of the finest works of literature the world has ever known, *every day* would feel like a gift, even a day spent in a Siberian labor camp.

And so it is for every Christian who understands the gospel— that God has established a way to bring forgiveness to us who deserve condemnation and death. We have been radically rescued and should be thankful for everything good that happens rather than sensitive to every unpleasant condition or situation that follows our conversion.

This major mindset shift has helped me weather disappointments while giving me increased gratitude for things I used to take for granted. This act of dismantling is the key to new joy and worship in our lives.

If I believe I deserve everything I think I'm entitled to regarding the world's recognition (respect, acclaim, affluence, and comfort) and get only 80 percent of that, *I'll feel poor.* I'll think I've been cheated of my rightfully remaining 20 percent. If I think I'm entitled to none of the world's respect, acclaim, affluence, and comfort and get 10 percent of that, *I'll feel rich.*

This is the secret of dismantling entitlement and learning rescue. What I think I deserve sets the standard for my own happiness. To properly worship God and to properly understand myself, I need to dismantle a sense of entitlement, and learn instead what it means that God has rescued me in the face of my desperate need for rescuing. He is the only one who could and did rescue me. He has already done his part and has no need to ever prove himself to me again. That attitude should shape me and define every cell of my physical and spiritual being.

I would have been offended earlier in my life if you had told me I felt entitled. But I was so deceived in entitlement's grip that I didn't understand how much it shaped my emotions, moods, and thinking. When I began thinking of myself as one who was rescued, the calcified-like encumbrance of an entitled spirit gradually began to lose its hold on me. I exchanged a deadened sense of frustration for a life-giving stream of joy and hope.

The journey from entitlement to rescue is a personal one, but to illustrate how widely it impacts everything we do, here's how it has changed my thinking: Instead of resenting it every time a flight is delayed or canceled, I'm thankful that modern air travel makes traveling possible to so many churches in one lifetime. Instead of being bitter that none of our children or grandchildren live near us, I'm deeply thankful we have children—and that FaceTime means we still get to "see" them and airplanes make it possible to visit them. Instead of being discouraged when a book I've written seems to be ignored, I realize I don't deserve the opportunity to write a single book, much less more than twenty. Instead of feeling slighted that I haven't been invited to speak at *that* church or *that* conference, I rejoice in God's unmerited favor that, despite my sin, I still get to speak at *any* church or conference. When I read of what soldiers went through during World War II winters, I feel blessed to sleep in my bedroom, even though the French doors need to be replaced for at least five reasons. As I face the bodily limitations of age, I'm overwhelmed with gratitude that God has granted me so many decades.

The rescued life resets our mindsets to that of those who have already won the spiritual lottery. We have been blessed far beyond what we deserve. Every blessing is a gift, and every deprivation is reduced by our salvation and hope and by the presence of God.

You and I were—and on our own, we still are—*helpless*. If you can't accept that, you can't accept Christianity. Jesus didn't come with a moral improvement program but with a death, resurrection, and re-creation invitation. No death? No new life.

Here's what I found once I exchanged my entitlement mindset for the identity of one who is rescued—joy, gratitude, and dependence that keep me from discouragement, doubt, and spiritual exhaustion. It's such a better life—this life of taking Jesus' yoke upon us and finding rest for our souls. I could finally die to the terrible weight of feeling like I wasn't getting what I deserve (indeed I wasn't, but not in the way I thought!) and instead appreciate every moment and every favor as a generous gift from God.

## ENTITLEMENT THINKING

Kaylin is thirty-five and single but wants to be married. She's in better shape physically than most of her friends. She is buying a house, loves the Lord, and carries on a conversation as skillfully as anyone. But she has started to blame God now: *I did everything I'm supposed to do, saving myself for marriage and not settling for a nonbelieving spouse. I've done my part, God. Why haven't you done yours and given me a husband?*

Jeff and Grace have been dedicated parents, taking their children to church until they left home for college, modeling and talking about faith at home. All four of their children asked to be baptized but two of them no longer attend church as adults, and one of them says she no longer believes. *Hey, God,* they are tempted to say, *what about the verse that tells us to train up a child in the way they should go and in the end they won't depart from it? We did that, and you haven't come through for us with our children.*

Josiah hates his job. Yes, it provides for his family, but it's not fulfilling. Most of his friends at least kind of like their jobs. *Why doesn't God provide me with a better one?*

Chip is bitter about constant calls from creditors. He'd never state it quite this way, but when I listen to him, I hear these words of entitlement: *I should be able to spend everything I earn, accumulate debt on my credit card, and forget about saving up for retirement or emergencies because the Bible says that God will provide for me.*

Cesar is angry that God didn't give him a break with law enforcement. Again, while this isn't a direct quote, it's an honest summary of his thinking: *I'm entitled to drink and then drive but not get a DUI because I don't do it that much and I didn't realize I was that drunk, and God, couldn't you have given me a break? I know people who have broken this law far more often than I have, and they never got caught.*

All of this is entitlement thinking, and it's among the worst attitudes a Christian can have. One of the most effective ways to crawl out from under it is to realize we have been rescued. Entitlement dies when we realize that God treats us far better than we deserve.

# WHAT WE'VE BEEN SAVED FROM

Understanding our bedrock spiritual poverty and how we offend God is the place where entitlement goes to die. In a particularly compelling section of his *Institutes of the Christian Religion*, John Calvin explains why we must be so explicit about all that Christ has rescued us from. Calvin's purported obsession with God's wrath is but the threshold to God's wondrous, virtually incomprehensible mercy. God didn't just forgive us for jaywalking or driving six miles over the speed limit; he stepped in when we faced the just condemnation of eternal damnation.

Calvin compares one man who is given only a general understanding of God's displeasure over his sins and the destruction that awaits him and then is told that God delivered him. The explicitness about *every* item of our peril and *every* aspect of Christ's rescue results in a much greater and more worshipful appreciation for the benefits we receive in Christ:

> Suppose he learns, as Scripture teaches, that he was estranged from God through sin, is an heir of wrath, subject to the cause of eternal death, excluded from all hope of salvation, beyond every blessing of God, the slave of Satan, captive under the yoke of sin, destined finally for a dreadful destruction and already involved in it; and that at this point Christ interceded as his advocate, took upon himself and suffered the punishment that, from God's righteous judgment, threatened all sinners; that he purged with his blood those evils which had rendered sinners hateful to God; that by this expiation he made satisfaction and sacrifice duly to God the Father; that as intercessor he has appeased God's wrath; that on this foundation rests the peace of God with men; that by this bond his benevolence is maintained toward them. Will the man not then be even more

moved by all these things which so vividly portray the greatness of the calamity from which he has been rescued?[2]

An honest portrayal of my spiritual condition is this: I was a mess in a mess, but God sent Jesus and now I have peace, hope, forgiveness, joy, and grace—none of which I deserve. Downplaying what we've been rescued from minimizes the importance of our rescue. It also undermines our worship of such a benevolent, kind, and powerful rescuer simply because we think we're not receiving what we deserve after we've been rescued.

Entitled people feel like God hasn't played fair with them. They think they've done their part but God hasn't done his. Sometimes they adopt general words spoken to nations in Scripture and claim them as absolute *personal* promises, all the while conveniently forgetting how indebted to God they are and always will be.

Let's take an honest look at what Scripture says we can rightfully expect from God.

## WHAT WE CAN EXPECT

Entitlement thinking thrives when we don't look at life as Scripture lays it out for us. We feel entitled because we think life should be a certain way, that God should treat us the way we want him to, and that we shouldn't have to face this thing or that thing. We need to dismantle this faulty thinking.

What does Scripture say we can and should expect?

- Our sin separates us from God (Isaiah 59:2).
- We deserve the wrath of God (Romans 1:18).

- We live in a fallen world where relationships will be hard (Genesis 3:16).
- Our struggle against sin will be fierce and ongoing (Romans 7:15ff.).
- The nonbelieving world will persecute us (John 15:18).
- Our bodies will get sick and experience physical death (1 Corinthians 15:42–44).

Jesus doubles down on this: "In this world you will have trouble. But take heart! I have overcome the world" (John 16:33). Jesus *promises* us that life will be full of trouble, but he also promises to be with us right in the very middle of that trouble.

What then does it mean to be transformed by the renewing of our minds (Romans 12:1–2)? It means we unlearn entitlement and accept the fact that life will be really hard but Jesus will walk with us every step of the way.

The apostle Paul set the bar for our expectations when he wrote, "If we have food and clothing, we will be content with that" (1 Timothy 6:8). This is a verse surprisingly few Christians learn or apply. We think Paul must be using hyperbole.

We want a certain kind of food, a certain kind of clothing, and if we're married, a certain kind of relatively happy marriage. And a certain kind of house. And the ability to go on vacation every now and then. We'd also appreciate being respected and thought of as "nice, good people" by the world at large. And a job that doesn't just give us the means to buy food and clothing, but one that uses our talents, allows us to grow, and is at least somewhat enjoyable.

To whatever degree we add to 1 Timothy 6:8 and reject John 16:33, we grow in our sense of entitlement. Our "rescued" attitude should be this: Life can be hard and disappointing, and this world is hostile, even if we love and serve Jesus (in fact, *especially* if we love and serve Jesus). But the spiritual riches I enjoy in Christ are overwhelmingly superior to anything I deserve. I consider myself to be one of God's most blessed creatures.

If this is challenging for you, print out the verses in this section—what we deserve and are promised—and then print out some of the forthcoming verses on the nature of Christ's rescue. Saturate your mind and soul with the truth that will set you free from an entitled mindset, so that you will cherish your status as one who has been rescued by Christ.

Here's the bonus for adopting this mindset: *When entitlement drops, happiness rises.*

Tough things will happen to us, regardless of whether we believe they should, but our emotions can take us to a different place. An entitled mentality leads us to say, *God, how dare you?* The rescued mentality holds to this bedrock truth (through which faith, joy, and endurance thrive): *God, you treat me better than I deserve.*

God doesn't promise me that my spouse will be faithful, so I have no reason to blame God if they aren't; God promises me that *he* will be faithful. God doesn't promise me that my boss will be fair or my kids will be grateful; he promises me that he will reward those who seek and serve him.

Most of the things that turn us away from God and make us angry at God come from entitlement thinking.

## ENTITLEMENT IS OUR ENTRY INTO SIN

In a Christian worldview, all sin is accompanied by grotesque entitlement. I cannot steal without entitlement ("If I want it, I'll take it").

I cannot murder ("If you displease me, you shouldn't even be alive"), gossip, commit adultery, oppress ("If I need to use you, I will"), or harm anyone without being fueled by entitlement. Even seemingly personal sins, like drunkenness, overeating, and bitter rumination, are based on the entitled attitude that my body and mind belong to me, not to God, and I can do whatever I want with them, thank you very much.

Mistreating my own body would be like stealing my rich dad's luxury car, going on a joyride, driving recklessly, carelessly running into a pole, totaling the car, and then casually walking away as I throw the keys into the ditch. All onlookers who discovered the details would say, "What a spoiled, entitled kid!"

God's Word guides us to the abundant life that is found through remaining within God's will. The commands of God are not capricious—that is, impulsively given with perhaps ill or angry motives—nor are they arbitrary. I've heard various teachers say many times, "Every sin has a consequence." Discipleship can feel like it has an exorbitant cost, but at least it's an investment with a huge payoff. And we buy disobedience at an even steeper cost—we gain so little and for such a short time, and it can cost us everything. Disobedience *fuels* pernicious entitlement. It isn't just corrupt; it is corrupt*ing*.

I have fallen into it. And so have you. If Satan, the accuser of believers (Revelation 12:10), were to create a lowlight reel of our worst acts and our most hostile motives, we'd all be ashamed of how entitled we have acted—and—let's be honest—continue to act. It's not just that I've *been* rescued; it's that I *still need* rescuing.

My sins as a believer are worse than those of nonbelievers because I know better, and I have the Holy Spirit to rely on. The only reason I sin is that I choose to—even though I know the truth and have been given power to resist temptation. Understanding not just my past guilt but my present guilt sets me up to find refuge in the only one who can rescue me from this morass—my Savior and Rescuer, Jesus Christ. And it utterly demolishes the spiritual morass of entitlement thinking.

## OUR GRACIOUS AND CAPABLE RESCUER

The apostle Paul eloquently presented the incomparably great power of Jesus' rescuing work:

> For he has rescued us from the dominion of darkness and brought us into the kingdom of the Son he loves, in whom we have redemption, the forgiveness of sins. (Colossians 1:13–14)

> What a wretched man I am! Who will rescue me from this body that is subject to death? Thanks be to God, who delivers me through Jesus Christ our Lord! (Romans 7:24–25)

> Grace and peace to you from God our Father and the Lord Jesus Christ, who gave himself for our sins to rescue us from the present evil age, according to the will of our God and Father, to whom be glory for ever and ever. (Galatians 1:3–5)

We're rescued not just from God's wrath but from "the present evil age." Let's go to seminary for just a few moments, shall we? Theologians typically identify two views of atonement to explain why Jesus died on the cross and what his death accomplished. In the West, the most common view is penal substitutionary atonement, which essentially teaches that Christ paid the ransom for our sin and rebellion; he was punished in our place so that we might be forgiven. I believe in penal substitutionary atonement because Scripture teaches it.*

The "Great Schism" took place in the eleventh century between the Eastern and Western branches of Christianity. While there were several issues at play, a big one revolved around the primacy of the Roman bishop as the supreme pontiff, or "pope." After the Great Schism, different emphases with regard to the atonement developed among Western and Eastern theologians. In Eastern theology, the purpose behind Christ's death is often summarized in the term "Christus Victor": In his death and resurrection, Jesus triumphed over the powers of evil, including sin, death, and the devil. We were powerless against these forces until Jesus died on our behalf to liberate us.

Theologians have sometimes pitted these two explanations against each other, but what if both are simultaneously true? I agree with the doctrine of penal substitutionary atonement—that I deserve God's wrath and need someone to remove it from me. I also agree with the Christus Victor view that I was a powerless victim who needed someone to rescue me from a battle I couldn't possibly win. (By the way, it isn't just the Eastern Orthodox perspective of atonement that exalts Christus Victor; Puritan Richard Baxter held that view as well.)

I believe that these two perceptions—that we deserve God's wrath and that we are victims who need to be rescued—can coexist and that in God's economy they do. Yes, we are guilty. In one sense, we are rescued from our very selves, as we are the captains of our own destruction. But we are also victims, caught up in an evil age that is smarter and more powerful than our ability to defeat. We are destined to be corrupted, led astray, deceived, and abused.

In Romans 3:9, Paul confessed that we are all "under the power of

---

* See Isaiah 53:6, 12; Romans 3:25–26; 2 Corinthians 5:21; and other Scripture passages.

sin." In Romans 7:14, he added that each one of us is "sold as a slave to sin." In his letter to the Galatians, he pointed out that "the Scriptures declare that we are all prisoners of sin, so we receive God's promise of freedom only by believing in Jesus Christ" (3:22 NLT).

I read these verses and think, *Lord, have mercy! I need to be rescued. This doesn't sound like a condition I can overcome on my own.* Far from it! We need someone more powerful to rescue us from overwhelmingly unbeatable odds.

It's possible for *Christus Victor* (Christ is the victor who rescues us from sin) to coexist with *penal substitution* (Christ absorbs the wrath of God poured out because of our sin) if both are presented in a complementary way. Eastern and Western expressions of Christianity can come together over the truth that we *are* victims who *are* objects of wrath. Christ's work is a more thorough rescue than either emphasis teaches on its own. I am rescued from my own sins and God's rightful wrath, and I am *also* rescued from the present evil age. I am a sinning perpetrator, and I have been sinned against. Both are true, and both require a rescue only Christ can provide.

Adopting a rescue mindset means I remind myself that I don't deserve grace. I don't deserve the presence of the Holy Spirit in my life. I don't deserve the promise of eternal salvation. I don't deserve the wisdom and truth of God's Word. I don't deserve the hope and the power God makes available to me through his Son and the Holy Spirit. I don't deserve the Father's acceptance and affirmation.

Not deserving any of that, *but given all of that,* anything else in life—including a house I like, a job I enjoy, and a spouse I cherish—is absolutely frosting on the cake, with extra sprinkles and a dash of undeserved happiness.

What I think I deserve sets the standard for my own happiness, which is why I believe that when entitlement drops, happiness rises.

I'm not suggesting we should feel guilty if God has blessed us abundantly, but rather that we should adopt a heart of gratefulness for every *small* blessing. This morning, as I finished my run, I found dozens of things to be thankful for. I get to run in a nice pair of Hokas. I have good sunglasses and a hat to cover my bald head. I get to wear tech gear and special running socks. God has given me health and a body that can still run. The weather was pleasant. And what a beautiful trail God has designed that I get to run on. I have an app on my phone that tracks my distance right down to the foot, earbuds through which I can listen to a good podcast, and safe passages all around me—no threats of war, robbery, or violence of any kind.

Listing all these things to be thankful for didn't feel like a duty; it made me deliriously happy, thankful, and worshipful.

And I don't deserve any of it. The reason I can be happy is that Jesus has reconciled me to my creator in spite of my rebellion.

Do you recognize your need to be rescued? Or do you think God hit the jackpot when you signed up to follow him? Have you learned how utterly ruined you would be without him?

Release and dismantle the sense of entitlement, which distorts and even perverts the way you look at God, yourself, and others. And then learn the new mindset that comes from realizing you have been rescued.

## THE JOYS OF A RESCUED MINDSET

If we view ourselves as Fyodor Dostoevsky did—as people on death row who are about to be executed but are saved at the last moment—we won't complain if someone has a larger platform than we do. *We'll be grateful we have any platform at all.* If you think of yourself as a

Dostoevsky condemned to die, and three of your four children are alienated from you, you'll be grateful for the relationship you have with the one instead of obsessing over what you don't have with the other three. Even if all of them are estranged, in one sense you'll be grateful that you are still alive and thus there is the possibility for reconciliation in the future—something a convicted and executed criminal would never have.

The rescue mindset is the path through which even a Siberian labor camp can feel like a place of abundance. When we look at the world through the lens of the gospel—what we deserve and what we've been saved from, and our heavenly Father's kind and generous intervention shown to us in Christ's death and resurrection—entitlement shrinks, grace abounds, and joy overflows.

A rescued mindset is a trusting mindset. What God has withheld from you could have, in fact, ruined you. William Law talked about the danger of worldly abundance and urged us to consider a man who, because of his riches, can and does live a debauched life. At the end of his life, looking back, he might wish he had been poor since he was unable to resist the temptations of being affluent. A woman may be "envied for her beauty" but in the end "owe all her misery to it," while another woman, looking back, "may be for ever happy for having had no admirers of her person." Law spoke of a clergyman who was ruined by being made a bishop, who would have been saved if he had remained at his "first poor vicarage." He compared the apostle Paul with Alexander the Great, who built towns, set up statues "and left marks of his glory in so many kingdoms! And how despised was the poor preacher St. Paul when he was beaten with rods! And yet how strangely was the world mistaken in their judgment! How much to be envied was St. Paul! How much to be pitied was Alexander!"[3]

# ENTITLED AFFLUENCE

As a pastor, my passion is to encourage people to pray David's marvelous prayer in Psalm 17:7: "Show me the wonders of your great love." Understanding God's love is a precursor to our ability and desire to love others (1 John 4:19). But we can't receive the wonders of God's great love if we are angry at God. Know this: More times than not (there are certainly exceptions), anger toward God stems from an entitled attitude. The entitled Christian prays, *God, why won't you answer all my prayers the way I want you to answer them?* The rescued Christian prays, *God, I know I deserve to be in hell. I praise you for your grace.*

This goes far beyond eternal destiny. Reading through Luke 10, I was struck by how, when Jesus sent out the seventy-two, he told them to stay wherever they were welcomed and to eat whatever was put before them, "for the worker deserves his wages" (v. 7). The "wages" they were entitled to was thus limited to a roof, not even a bed, and a meal, however simple. There's no mention of a single luxury—truly just the bare necessities.

Anything else is a gift.

I can't prove it, but when Jesus added, "Do not move around from house to house," I think he may have been saying, *Don't try to upgrade. Spend your time ministering, not worrying about your surroundings.*

Affluence has blanketed our expectations of what we are to receive and how we are to be treated to the point that we stand on the precipice of losing our sense of wonder regarding God's great love and spiritual provisions and instead become angry at our heavenly Father for withholding earthly luxuries. Two thousand years ago, people must have been fixated on getting enough to eat and an extra set of clothes. Jesus sought to relieve them of that worry: "Do not set your heart on what you will eat or drink; do not worry about it. For the pagan world runs after all such things, and your Father knows that you need them. But seek his kingdom, and these things will be given to you as well" (Luke 12:29–31).

Most of today's believers—in the West anyway—don't have to worry about not having enough to eat or about walking around in tattered clothing. The things that keep us from seeking the kingdom are a *better* car, a *bigger* house, a more exotic vacation, a more upscale restaurant, and a club membership. If we accepted Paul's maxim—"If we have food and clothing, we will be content with that" (1 Timothy 6:8)—we'd have an entirely different ruler by which to measure our sense of entitlement.

I've met enough faithful believers with lifetime health conditions that I don't take a day without pain or discomfort for granted. God has rescued me from pain, even while letting others live in it. When I was a young boy, I was playing backyard football with my friends. I went in for a headfirst tackle and stung my neck. For an instant, my neck felt electrified, and I thought something could be seriously wrong. Time almost stopped. I had this initial feeling like in a movie where the background gets blurry and the sound goes silent and you think, *Everything has changed.*

But then I was fine.

This may sound weird, but I've always had a sense, though I can't rationally explain it and don't want to argue about it, that God rescued me in that moment from what could have been a lifelong injury. I'll find out for sure when I get to heaven, but I still believe God let me evade the foolishness of my choice to throw myself headfirst into a bigger boy's knees just to stop him from getting a touchdown in a back-yard game that didn't matter. I've never forgotten that the privilege of being a runner, having a relatively healthy body, playing with my kids, hugging my wife, driving a car, traveling on my own—it's all a bonus, all a gift. By all rights, I should have lived my life in a wheelchair.

God rescued me. The truth is, throughout my life, he has rescued me from things I didn't think I needed to be rescued from. Rescued from financial excess at an early age? Rescued from being too handsome? Rescued from being too famous? Rescued from accruing too much power? I never prayed to be rescued from any of these, but I can see how any one of them, and certainly all of them together, could well have ruined me many times over. As it is, I love God more in my sixties than I have at any time in my life, and I thought I was passionately in love with God in my twenties. I am more zealous for his kingdom, more grateful for his fellowship, and more in awe of who he is.

Who knows but that a different life with fewer disappointments and more earthly successes could have taken that away. I see some people, once zealous for God, who aren't even sure they believe in him anymore, and I shudder. Thank God that he rescued me from the multitude of things I once craved!

God saved me from more than a broken neck. Much more. He saved me from a calloused soul and an apathetic heart. And he alone is the rescuer who repeatedly has put my feet on solid ground in spite of my wandering heart.

Dismantle entitlement and learn what it means to live in the beautiful reality that you have been rescued.

# 12

# DISMANTLING COMPLACENT IGNORANCE

## *Learn the Value of Wisdom*

*We do, however, speak a message of wisdom among
the mature, but not the wisdom of this age or of the
rulers of this age, who are coming to nothing.*

1 CORINTHIANS 2:6

*The one who gets wisdom loves life;
the one who cherishes understanding will soon prosper.*

PROVERBS 19:8

I wanted to qualify for the Boston Marathon about as much as I have
ever wanted to do anything in my life. When I hit my mid-forties, I

figured it was time to go for it, so I lost weight. I ran speed workouts. I ran long distances, which in the Pacific Northwest sometimes meant running two hours in nonstop rain. I failed to run a fast enough qualifier in my first three attempts but finally got to the place in my fitness where I thought I might be able to do this.

During my fourth marathon, I hit mile twenty-five with sixteen minutes to spare. Sixteen minutes to run one mile (I had been averaging 7:45 miles), and I was in! I started to get dizzy—really dizzy—and pleaded nonstop with God, *Please don't let me pass out. I'm almost there!*

I crossed the line in 3:22—eight minutes to spare—and saw my name listed on the finishers sheet with the coveted "BQ" (Boston Qualifier) next to it.

And then the race director shattered our hearts when he said, "I guarantee you that the course is 26.2 miles, but we had to make some last-minute changes to the course to accommodate road improvements. While I am 100 percent confident of the course's length, we didn't have time to get a proper legal verification, so our marathon can't be used as a Boston qualifier this year."

I had done the work. I had suffered the pain. I had run the race. But it was all for naught because I ran the wrong course. Fortunately, I repeated the effort in the Seattle Marathon a few months later and achieved the qualification, but what if I hadn't? I had invested so much effort and time and endured a ton of pain, but if you don't run a verified course, none of that matters to the Boston officials.

In what life goals have you invested much effort and energy? A certain kind of family? A certain academic or vocational achievement? What if at the end of your life, you find out that you ran the wrong race? You neglected to run the course that counted, the one that really mattered?

King Solomon observed that many people exert a lot of effort in life.

They chase many goals with diligence, working hard and sacrificing to achieve them, but at the end of their lives, they are going to discover that they have run the wrong race. I invested many months—actually years—in my pursuit of my running goal. But what if at the end of your life, you realized you had spent *decades* pursuing lesser things?

The pursuit of an ever-increasing wisdom is supremely valued in Scripture. We need to dismantle our complacency about being wise enough and learn the need to pursue more wisdom every day. There's a reason this is the last chapter in the book: It reinforces the dismantling and relearning process we've been talking about all along.

## SOLOMON'S SECRET TO SUCCESS

The beginning of wisdom is this: Get wisdom.
    Though it cost all you have, get
understanding.
Cherish her, and she will exalt you;
    embrace her, and she will honor you.
She will give you a garland to grace your head
    and present you with a glorious crown.
    (Proverbs 4:7–9)

Solomon warned us that if our lives aren't marked by a never-ending pursuit for *more* wisdom and understanding, we are running the wrong course. And the very beginning of wisdom and understanding—next to fearing God (Proverbs 9:10)—is wanting unreservedly to be wiser and more understanding than we already are. Even if we're wiser today than we were five years ago, we should seek to be wiser yet five years from today.

The truth is, most of us don't passionately pursue wisdom because we're comfortable with where we are in life. We think we know enough. We're getting by with what we have, and so many more compelling pursuits capture our imagination. We need to shun this complacency—thinking that the wisdom we possess is sufficient—and learn instead to be hungry and thirsty and willing to sacrifice to obtain even more of this supremely valuable spiritual treasure.

If we don't earnestly pursue wisdom, we won't get wiser, because it doesn't happen by coincidence. There's a price to be paid: "*Though it cost all you have*, get understanding," wrote Solomon (Proverbs 4:7, emphasis added). Add up everything else you own, and none of it is as useful or worthwhile to you as wisdom.

John Bevere shares a powerful analogy: "If someone told you there were ten million dollars hidden somewhere in your home, you would search for it nonstop until you found the hidden fortune. If need be, you would pull up carpets, rip open drywall, and even tear the house down to the foundation in order to find that much money."[1] That's the kind of determination we need in our pursuit of wisdom. If we knew how valuable it is, we wouldn't stop tearing apart our lives and schedules to get it.

Wisdom is more important than your house, your car, your wardrobe, or your retirement account. "How much better to get wisdom than gold, to get insight rather than silver!" (Proverbs 16:16).

Getting such wisdom may cost you some sleep. It will definitely cost you some screen time. It may feel like work. But Solomon promised that wisdom will exalt everyone who cherishes her and honor everyone who embraces her.

In fact, wisdom is so powerful a possession that pursuing it is considered an act of self-love: "To acquire wisdom is to love yourself; people who cherish understanding will prosper" (Proverbs 19:8 NLT).

## THE HIGHWAY TO WISDOM

Though meaningful podcasts, sermons, lectures, and documentaries can help us grow in wisdom and understanding, one of the best ways to strengthen our minds and gain understanding is by reading. I caught my son reading a lengthy book on vacation that didn't seem to coincide with the graduate studies he was undertaking. Knowing how many books he had to read during and before the school year, I was intrigued to know why he was reading yet another book and asked him about it.

By way of background, some of the most influential and successful people in the world speak as guest lecturers at his graduate school. Graham has heard heads of states, business titans, professional athletes, politicians, entertainers, you name it. When I asked about the book he was reading, he told me, "I've noticed something about every super-successful person we've heard speak at school."

"What's that?"

"They all read a lot of books and watch only a little bit of television."

Graham's perspective is a shared one. Charlie Munger, cofounder of Berkshire Hathaway with Warren Buffett, once said, "In my whole life, I have known no wise people (over a broad subject area) who didn't read all the time—none."[2]

It's not just business or investment titans that hold this perspective. I read a book on preaching that was written several decades ago. One small section featured a dynamic pastor in Houston, Texas, who was knocking it out of the park on a weekly basis with captivating sermons that would eventually generate one of the largest churches in the nation.

The author asked the pastor how he managed to consistently preach sermon after sermon like he did. It's one thing to occasionally make people sit up and take notice, but week after week? This pastor, Dr. Ed Young, didn't give the writer what he was hoping for. Perhaps the interviewer expected the ten commandments of sermon writing. Maybe he wanted to know the six keys to preparing gripping sermons.

Dr. Young gave him just four words:

I read a lot.

If you're aiming for success in life, business, or ministry, reading good books must become a daily practice.

For the Christian, reading begins with God's Word—both Old and New Testaments. Because the Bible is so widely available, we can take for granted the resource that often lies unused in our houses, like a man or woman married to a beautiful spouse, or a sports beat reporter who nightly reports on the most gifted athletes alive today. The wow factor fades, but it's to our serious detriment if that should ever happen to be the case with Scripture.

In a Good Friday letter, Pastor Mike Woodruff noted, "Christ's words on the cross came from Psalm 22. This was not the first time he quoted Scripture. When he was tempted in the wilderness, he countered every one of Satan's assaults with passages from Deuteronomy. And while he was carrying the cross down the Via Dolorosa, he cited Hosea. The Word of God (incarnate) was so saturated in the Word of God (written) that it shaped his thoughts and words, even in times of great stress."[3]

Go back nearly five hundred years to the middle of the seventeenth century, when Scripture wasn't nearly as accessible as it is today. Anglican clergyman William Gurnall quoted Matthew 11:28 ("Come to me, all you who are weary and burdened") and said that we "had better be without meat, drink, light, air, earth, life, and all, than without this one comfortable scripture."[4] He went on to give several colorful illustrations about how his contemporaries and predecessors valued Scripture: "There are more riches and treasure to be had in one promise than all the gold and silver of the Indies is worth. . . . They are, in a word, the fair havens and safe road into which the tempted soul puts his weather-beaten ship, where it lies secure till the heavens clear, and the storms are over, which the world, sin, and Satan raise upon him."[5]

Gurnall lived within a century of William Tyndale, who was murdered for translating Scripture in his quest to make it approachable to the average layperson. Prior to Tyndale, John Hus was burned alive in 1415, and though John Wycliffe (who died in 1384) was imprisoned and persecuted but not executed for making the Bible accessible, religious authorities burned his bones to make sure what they called his "damnable heresy" couldn't be venerated.

Brave men and women died to give us the Scriptures that often collect dust in our homes. If I had lived my entire life with just one chapter from John's gospel and then Jesus visited me and handed me all four Gospels, with the accounts of his words, acts, and miracles in them, I would weep with joy and stop whatever I was doing in order to read them, meditate on them, and talk about them.

But since Jesus gave us these Gospels (by inspiring faithful servants) two thousand years ago, we forget how precious they are, how life-giving they are, how thankful we should be to have them, and how shameful it is to ignore them.

We have more than just Scripture, of course; we have the Holy Spirit to help us understand and apply its wisdom.* In two instances following Jesus' resurrection, Luke tells of how Jesus opened the minds of his followers to come to an understanding of Scripture (Luke 21:32, 45).

When we value this truth, start to feed off it, and learn to be

---

* Paul wrote, "This is what we speak, not in words taught us by human wisdom but in words taught by the Spirit, explaining spiritual realities with Spirit-taught words. The person without the Spirit does not accept the things that come from the Spirit of God but considers them foolishness, and cannot understand them because they are discerned only through the Spirit" (1 Corinthians 2:13–14).

comforted and inspired by it, we will feel like the richest people on earth.

I bristle whenever I hear popular pastors warn about bibliolatry, as if we give too much reverence to Scripture today. I know there's a potential danger of acting as though we follow a book rather than a living God, but in general, you'll find ninety-nine Christians underutilizing Scripture for every one person who idolizes it.

When it comes to Scripture, we must dismantle the notion that we already "know enough." We can never know enough. We need to keep studying these miraculous, life-giving words. I don't know how many times I've read the Bible—I'm guessing it's dozens of times. But the more I read these familiar stories, the more I get out of them. They never stop instructing, challenging, correcting, encouraging, and inspiring me.

## HEAD AND HEART

There's a sad and mistaken strain of faith that sees head knowledge as inferior to heart change. The Bible doesn't put one over the other, and neither should we. Jesus said, "You will know the truth, and the truth will set you free" (John 8:32). The head can lead, inform, and guard the heart, while the heart is essential to keep the head thinking straight. When our passions go awry, we can convince ourselves of anything. The head and the heart complement each other; they are not competitors.

When it comes to revivals—great outpourings of ministry and a widespread response to the Word of God—most people think the key is prayer. "Pray, pray, pray," they'll say, and I agree. Prayer is powerful, and it is commanded. It must be a daily staple for passionate believers.

But what if there's more to revival than prayer?

John Wesley was involved in the Great Awakening, one of the

most widespread revivals in American history. He certainly prayed with fervor, but there was another important element behind such a historically significant work of God: Wesley and his followers read voraciously. In fact, he read many of his books while riding on horseback as he traveled from town to town. Much later in life, when he finally had to begin traveling in a carriage, the first thing he did was to board up one side of the carriage to make a bookcase out of it.[6]

If you were a circuit-riding Methodist preacher during Wesley's lifetime, you were expected to awaken at four in the morning to read Scripture together for about an hour. Then after breakfast, their practice was to read from six until noon from what Wesley called the "Christian Library," great books of the faith that he thought every Christian should read.

Wesley's brilliance in launching such a far-reaching movement was simple: You can't give out what you don't first take in. Otherwise, your ministry will resemble a fire that is fed by paper; it may flare up immediately, but it will burn out faster than you can imagine.

You may not be called to be a circuit-riding preacher, but are you a parent? A friend? A boss? A colleague? A grandparent? An evangelist? If you want to give more to those you love, become ravenously hungry to take in more.

## READ MORE THAN YOU WATCH

If we want to experience a more abundant life in business or ministry, here's a simple rule: Read more than you watch. That's what the best minds do.

A 2015 study published in the journal *Cerebral Cortex* found that watching too much TV alters the composition of the human brain (and now we can add the impact that social media screen time has on the brain):

- It lowers IQ.
- It frustrates language acquisition.
- It increases psychological difficulties (stress, anxiety, depression).
- It reduces attention.
- It reduces our ability to manage anger.[7]

Reading, by contrast, strengthens neural pathways. A study published in *Neurology* found that steady and consistent reading throughout life fights against cognitive decline as we age.[8] A Sussex University study found that reading is also the surest path to relaxation. Even six minutes of reading at the end of the day can do wonders to help your body de-stress. In just 360 seconds, participants' heart rates had slowed and muscles began to relax. Reading tested out as more effective in this regard than listening to music, drinking a cup of tea, playing video games, or taking a walk.[9]

The lifelong pursuit of wisdom is more important than amassing power. Solomon, who had been gifted with substantial power throughout his life, wrote, "Better a poor but wise youth than an old but foolish king who no longer knows how to heed a warning" (Ecclesiastes 4:13). It's better to be young and poor with wisdom than old and powerful without it. If you have more time and more money but less wisdom, you are teetering on the edge of a tragic fall. An abundance of money and time will accentuate and enable your foolishness, making a sad end more likely than not.

Of course, we must apply what we learn. Absolutely, there's a problem with "head knowledge" that doesn't transform but simply puffs us up. The solution, however, isn't pursuing wisdom less; it's pursuing application more.

Reading was a favored path to wisdom by none other than the apostle Paul. You'll recall his famous plea from 2 Timothy 4:13: "When you come, bring the cloak that I left with Carpus at Troas, and my scrolls, especially the parchments."

What makes me smile when I read this verse is Paul's humility. If I had written Romans, the two Corinthian letters, Galatians, Ephesians, and Colossians, I can't imagine wanting to read anything written by anyone else. I think I'd just memorize my own writings. What more is there to learn? His books are inspired genius. One sentence can occupy my mind for weeks on end. Consider Philippians 2:3: "Do nothing out of selfish ambition"—six words that can change a life focus. Or for husbands, Ephesians 5:25: "Husbands, love your wives, just as Christ loved the church and gave himself up for her." If you spend a lifetime trying to wring every bit of wisdom out of that power-packed sentence, it still won't be enough.

Yet a man who could throw out gems like this kept mining for more jewels from other people's mountains. We don't know for sure what scrolls and parchments Paul requested, but most scholars think they included (but weren't limited to) portions of what now makes up the New Testament. Think about what this means: Even those who *wrote* the Bible *read* the Bible. We know for sure that Peter read Paul's letters (2 Peter 3:16). If you think you are already wise enough or smart enough not to need books, you're placing yourself above the apostles.

Commenting on 2 Timothy 4:13, Charles Spurgeon wrote these words:

[Paul] is inspired, and yet he wants books! He has been preaching at least for thirty years, and yet he wants books! He has seen the

Lord, and yet he wants books! He had had a wider experience than most men, and yet he wants books! He had been caught up into the third heaven, and had heard things which it was unlawful for a man to utter, yet he wants books! He had written the major part of the New Testament, and yet he wants books![10]

If Paul needed books and Peter needed books, how do we not need books?

## TRANSFORMATION

It is difficult for me to write a book without quoting Matthew 6:33 or Romans 12:2 (I can see my wife's eyes rolling as I type this). But Romans 12:2 helps us understand why Paul saw reading as the preferred path to an abundant life when he wrote the famous words we've already quoted: "Do not conform to the pattern of this world, but be transformed *by the renewing of your mind*" (emphasis added).

Every word in this sentence (and even the comma) is worthy of study. It's a masterpiece. We don't have space in this chapter to do a deep dive, but a few elements beg to be acknowledged as we pursue life in Christ. First, Paul warned that we must actively fight against being "conformed" to the "pattern of this world." Groupthink (popular consensus) is the enemy of life in Christ; it's precisely what we need to unlearn.

Here's the powerful takeaway: To do nothing is to be conformed. If we don't fight *against* being conformed, we *will* be conformed. If we consume popular culture mindlessly—its blog posts, podcasts, television series, movies, music, news, and commercial novels—we'll be conformed to popular culture. Remember, this age has an agenda, which is to run as fast as it can from God's agenda.

How many times have we seen historical dramas that integrate sinful actions and relationships into historical characters when we know those characters didn't do what they were being portrayed as doing? Why is the entertainment industry so relentless in injecting today's sins into yesterday's society? Don't you think it's possible there's an agenda behind that? You think you're simply being entertained; spiritual forces know you are being shaped by the "rulers . . . authorities . . . powers of this dark world and . . . the spiritual forces of evil in the heavenly realms" (Ephesians 6:12). How do we protect ourselves from this spiritual warfare? With the "belt of *truth*" (v. 14, emphasis added).

Our minds exist in a river of a society headed in one direction. If we don't paddle in the opposite direction, we'll be carried downstream. Living in a fallen world, we won't "happen upon" divine wisdom. We must seek it out. We must evaluate the source. The books and lectures promoted and exalted by the world may at times throw out a few nuggets of wisdom (I read plenty of "non-Christian" books), but we must realize that worldly wisdom is like eating trout. We have to spit out many bones to find the nourishing meat within.

In Paul's view, the world is shaping us and trying to squeeze us into its mold. It may use shame ("How dare you disagree with us?"), entertainment ("Don't worry about all that serious stuff; just let yourself escape for a while"), or head-on attack ("If you don't agree with us, we will ruin you"). It won't leave us alone.

How do we fight back against the pull to "conform to the pattern of this world"? Paul said we *use our minds*. In essence, he gave us an ultimatum: Either the world shapes us, or we shape ourselves. If we're not actively shaping our minds, we are passively allowing the world to shape them.

# THE RIGHT OBSESSION

During a 2015 performance of the Broadway play *Hand to God*, a young member of the audience became alarmed when he realized his cell phone was about to run out of power. He noticed an outlet on the stage and thought he could climb up on stage and plug in his phone. He must have thought no one would notice, but of course everybody did. There were boos, catcalls, and a momentary interruption. Veteran theatergoers knew it was a fool's errand to begin with—the outlet was part of a stage prop; it wasn't even connected to any power.

We live in a day and age when we are tempted to become obsessed with battery life. If you ask me at any given hour of the day, I could offer a fairly accurate estimate of how much battery life is left on my smartphone or tablet. If I'm having dinner at a close friend's house, I might even ask to plug in my phone while we eat. At church "greenrooms," one of my first glances is to find an open outlet to recharge my tablet between teaching sessions.

I wish we were as obsessed with brainpower as we are with battery power. If we understand the invitation behind Solomon's glorious challenge to gain wisdom, to seek understanding, we will recognize the need to continually develop our intellectual fitness. Yet many of us miss the ever-deepening glory of life in Christ because our priorities lie in different places. We don't value wisdom and understanding like Solomon did. We're more concerned about what the scale tells us about our weight, what our 401(k) statements (or the absence of them) tell us about our net worth, what Netflix or Hulu tells us is available to stream, or how much battery power is left in our latest gadget than we are with boosting our mental firepower with greater understanding.

With that in mind, let me give you one more motivation to embrace abundance via the path of reading: If you're negligent at all in this regard, you may have a pleasant surprise ahead of you—a brand-new you with vastly increased influence.

## THE NEW YOU

Precisely because reading is becoming more of a lost art, you can capitalize on the ignorance of others. That sentence will sound terrible if you read it with the motives and ethics of Machiavelli, but if you read it with the determination to "seek first the kingdom of God," it's an opportunity to influence others *for good*.

If you're not reading regularly, you don't yet know what you can be. You are an untapped and somewhat unformed spiritual commodity. You're like a potentially gifted athlete who has never trained, a genetically favored musician who has never picked up an instrument, or a born leader who lives in isolation.

In an attempt to encourage young people to lay hold of their potential, former First Lady Michelle Obama once told a group of young women how unimpressed she was with those who hold high office and wield wide influence in today's world: "I have been at probably every powerful table that you can think of, I have worked at nonprofits, I have been at foundations, I have worked in corporations, served on corporate boards, I have been at G-summits, I have sat in at the U.N.: They are not that smart."[11]

Her message is this: Don't limit yourself. Refuse to think you don't belong in that league. My message is this: If you want to be raised up to that place of influence, one of the surest ways to get there is by reading.

In 2007, billionaire investor Charlie Munger told a crowd of graduating law students at USC Gould School of Law, "I constantly see people rise in life who are not the smartest, sometimes not even the most diligent. But they are learning machines. They go to bed every night a little wiser than they were that morning. And boy, does that habit help, particularly when you have a long run ahead of you."[12]

If you're married but never read marriage books, if you're a parent but never read parenting books, if you're a Christian but never read spiritual formation books, if you're a leader but never read leadership books, you're putting a hard ceiling on your own development. You're limiting yourself to what you've already learned and sabotaging future advancement.

Years ago, I gave a talk on sex at a Sacred Marriage conference, and the pastor later told me that a couple in their seventies had visited him several weeks afterward, telling him that they were experiencing a second honeymoon in the bedroom. The wife had grown up with an unbiblical view of sex. One seventy-five-minute talk spurred an understanding that made her want to enjoy an aspect of marriage that had been neglected for too long. It also made her feel bitter about all the "lost years" (as she put it) she had never gotten to enjoy.

Many of us know the benefits of reading, and some of us know we waste time every day that could be better spent reading. What we need is what one writer calls "a fortress of habits" to discipline ourselves to lay hold of this aspect of abundant living.[13] My own "fortress" consists of getting up early to read. I begin with Scripture, then read something from one of the Christian classics, and then read a chapter of a contemporary Christian book. I read other books throughout the day as part of my study preparation, and at night, for entertainment, I mix up commercial novels, literary novels, biographies, history, and even the occasional business book. The morning "fortress" sets the tone for my day, however, as I want to start out as far ahead as I can on the "reading versus watching" scoreboard.

The other thing that helps me is having a goal. My own goal will seem slim to some and aggressive to others, but I shoot for completing fifty books a year. The problem is that some of these books (like one of Shelby Foote's Civil War volumes or N. T. Wright's theological tomes) can reach six hundred pages or more. I don't get too caught up in the overall number of pages, as I might read four novels that together take far less time to read than one scholarly volume. But having some kind of numerical count motivates me in the same way that people make lists and like to cross things off.

Reading is difficult for many people. Audiobooks and the abundance of good sermons and lectures now available for listening online provide many opportunities to enhance your understanding.

## THE FALL AND RISE OF EUROPE

The downfall that comes from devaluing reading and no longer pursuing wisdom leads to the demise of our character and culture. Gaining wisdom isn't just about smarts; even more important, it's about integrity, character, and abundant living. Dallas Willard wrote, "To serve God well we must think straight; and crooked thinking, unintentional or not, always favors evil."[14]

First-century Rome was so civilized, powerful, and full of life, art, laughter, power, and politics that it's shocking how quickly and how far it fell by the end of the fifth century, but here's what happened: The barbarians—the Huns, Goths, and Visigoths—conquered and destroyed not just people but also a civilization to the point where by the sixth century, Europeans were all but illiterate and without libraries.

What brought Europe back? A small and faithful band of devout monks copied and recopied every written thing they could find. They reintroduced literacy and books to Europe's population and thus slowly built civilization back up through reading and education.

In a day and age in which intellectual and moral barbarians seem to be taking over and unleashing a shallow and shame-based groupthink that sees God as the problem rather than the solution, we need to counteract lazy thinking with the more rigorous and more precise thinking of wisdom and understanding. Who will be today's Dorothy Sayers, C. S. Lewis, or G. K. Chesterton?

Some historical beliefs that elements of the Christian community held in the past shouldn't be defended. History is not perfect, nor is biblical interpretation. But the authority and relevance of Scripture and God's revelation to us, properly interpreted and understood, point to our surest road back to an abundant mind, life, church, nation, and world. Even more, it is the key to life in Christ and the life we were reborn to live.

Twenty-five years ago, I used to be encouraged as a writer when I flew on airplanes. Back then, 90 percent of the people sitting on a plane read books. There was just one movie offered for watching, and the technology to store and stream movies on a laptop didn't yet exist. Today, the numbers appear to be reversed: Ninety percent of air passengers are watching something or playing a video game on a mobile device. While depressing in what this might mean for the future of our culture, it can be encouraging to those who embrace life in Christ by pointing out that we can have an outsized influence. This gap opens wide the doors to the 10 percent who will yet embrace a daily passionate pursuit of wisdom and understanding.

Here is the reason this is the last chapter before the epilogue: The practice of dismantling lies and distractions is something we need to carry forward. It never stops. If we are transformed by the renewing of our minds, we must continue to renew our minds. Let's grab hold of some words well worth repeating:

The beginning of wisdom is this: Get wisdom.
    Though it cost all you have, get understanding.
Cherish her, and she will exalt you;
    embrace her, and she will honor you.
She will give you a garland to grace your head
    and present you with a glorious crown. (Proverbs 4:7–9)

# EPILOGUE

Thank you for taking this journey with me. You've probably noticed it has been a very personal one for me. Each one of these truths, on its own, has represented significant changes in my life—my perspective, joy, peace, and security. Together they represent the dawn of a new spiritual life. I say *dawn* because I have by no means mastered them. As I just observed, dismantling is a lifelong process.

Our protest against the great illusion and distractions of this world won't be accomplished in a Saturday march. It will require a *lifelong* commitment to new learning, surrender, and discoveries. This book can get you going, but it represents just the first mile in a marathon. When Paul urged us to stop allowing ourselves to be conformed, but rather continue to let ourselves be transformed, the "transformation is not something which is brought about in an instant," wrote C. E. B. Cranfield. "It has to be continually repeated, or, rather, it is a process which has to go on all the time the Christian is in this life."[1]

This age won't stop trying to conform us just because we decide to stop being conformed. It has dealt with rebels before and has the potential to overwhelm them with its loud opposition. To be born into this world *and to continue to live in this world* means some force is desperate to shape us. Cranfield wrote, "The good news, to which the imperative [do not be conformed] bears witness, is that they are no longer the helpless victims of tyrannizing forces, but are able to resist this pressure which comes both from without and from within, because God's merciful action in Christ has provided the basis of resistance."[2] Refusing to be conformed "must ever be a great part of the content of Christian exhortation, so long as the Church is 'militant here in earth.' For the pressures to conformity are always present, and always strong and insidious—so that the Christian often yields unconsciously."[3]

This is my plea for you not to put this book down and think the dismantling is over. It needs to be our life's passion. Gerrit Scott Dawson provides this counsel:

> It takes tremendous discipline to hold onto the truth that has been revealed to us. Without constant attention, our minds and hearts follow the worldview of the culture around us. We go with its flow automatically unless we are consciously swimming against the stream. . . . The further from the mainstream of contemporary thought a piece of the gospel narrative is, the more difficult it is to maintain in our minds as a coherent part of our worldview.[4]

To this end, I think this would be the kind of book best read and discussed in a small group.

Let's briefly review what we've discussed:

1. How I treasure peace! And how I see the life aims, passions, and lusts that compete with peace as far too costly. Pursuing them is just not worth it. For me, the thought that I could have peace *right now*—without having or achieving anything else—is one of the most precious truths for the spiritual life in Christ. Peace is found in resting in God our Shepherd, not in trying to fix the broken things in our lives.

2. I now realize that the desire to control my days and my life, and especially the reactions of others, is similar to trying to dig through a

steel wall with a plastic spoon. Why play a game you can never win? When we try to control what we can't control, we bring only agony, frustration, and simmering anger into our lives. When we turn things upside down and see the lack of control as a blessed adventure instead of a terrifying curse—well, the very thing that once brought agony now brings joy. Amazing!

3. I don't know whether anyone has tried harder (or wanted it more) to make family life work. That sounds like a profoundly arrogant thing to say, so I'm sure it's not true, but pursuing the perfect family formed the fiber of my being. When I embraced the fact that the Trinity is my truest family, I could accept, serve, and enjoy my earthly family all the more.

4. As an introvert, I didn't think I needed community as much as others did, in the same way that someone living in a sunny climate is less likely to need a vitamin D supplement. But *thinking* I needed it less obscured the fact that I actually needed it just as much—maybe not in the same quantity but certainly in the same quality. I have been truly blessed accordingly. Relationships have brought abundant joy in this season of my life. While I treasure spiritual solitude, I watch out for the independently driven diversions that lead to an increasingly isolated life.

5. Though it seems plain to me now, abandoning my early childhood belief that being a Christian was all about my journey to get into heaven and realizing that the point of the gospel is that Jesus died so we would live as he lived—not for our own interests, but to advance the kingdom of God—has given me a much bigger life. And I'm glad I learned this before the allure of retirement and self-centeredness eclipsed potential years of fruitfulness.

6. Archbishop Fulton Sheen wrote, "To a man who has never rooted the soul in the Divine every trouble exaggerates itself."[5] That

was the story of my life when I craved comfort. I thought I was so heavenly minded, and yet all the while I was exaggerating and focusing on every earthly curse. It was all a mirage. Learning that God uses adversity and disappointment to color my soul, just as a master painter creates shades of light no one has ever seen before, makes each day a startling discovery of originality and wonder.

7. I hate my sin, but I love my Savior. Learning that I will never not need the Savior—not just for what I've done, but for what I am doing and will yet do—forcibly yanks my focus toward the supreme Redeemer and Savior, Jesus Christ. Accepting the ongoing reality of my struggle against sin not only changes the way I look at myself and what I expect from myself, but it also opens me up to receiving and learning from others who struggle with sin. There are very few people I cancel in my life anymore or write off permanently. Our God is a God of resurrection who wakes up the dead, even those we may (sort of) wish would stay dead.

8. As it was for the apostle Paul, I want one of my life-defining statements to be this: "He worked hard for the church." This goal is giving me new zeal and purpose, as well as lifting me out of embarrassment for and judgmentalism of the church. It has led me to fall deeply in love with the bride of Christ and learn how to appreciate her beauty instead of magnifying her faults in my attempt to prove that "I'm not one of *them*." How much better it is to love someone than to hate, criticize, or belittle them—especially someone loved, adored, and cherished by Christ!

9. Feeling for the first time a spiritually malignant force ("You are not welcome here") was sobering, but learning that I am surrounded by loving, powerful, and benevolent spiritual forces has been a new revelation for me. Though I've shared it here, I'm not sure if I yet understand the profound implications of all that this experience means. Many of

you are very likely further along this road, but I'm glad and grateful to God that I have at least started to walk on it.

10. When I finished the chapter on earthly splendor and how important it is to trade it all for the life that is rich toward God, I had to take a walk. It shook my soul that hard. I want this truth to define me, to set me free, to redirect me. Comparing Paul to Agrippa was an eye-opening lesson for me, compelling me to stop caring about what I used to care about and to refocus on what I formerly was blind to or at least paid too little attention to. It has given me an entirely new life. I may never taste a glass of Romanée-Conti wine, but I want to drink deeply of a life that is rich toward God.

11. Embracing the truth that I have been rescued and rejecting the lies that I am entitled have killed heaps of envy and bitterness in my life and completely remodeled my ambition and my expectations. It has launched a new season of joy, gratitude, and even exuberance for me. I truly hope it will do the same for you.

12. Finally, I commit anew to embracing the need for wisdom. Though I placed this topic in the last chapter, it's probably the one I learned earliest, through my sheer delight in reading the Scriptures and the insights of those who reflect on them. New insight thrills me; new learning feeds me; wisdom makes me feel so much stronger spiritually, like a person who lived a sedentary life and six months later got into physical shape and thought, *Why didn't I do this years ago?*

These thoughts have become my friends, and for you I hope they will become lifelong companions too, as together we climb out of the shackles of being conformed to the spirit of this age and are liberated to be transformed through the renewing of our minds.

# ACKNOWLEDGMENTS

I t may sound pretentious to say this, but thank you, Jesus. Without you none of this would matter.

I'm grateful to the team at Zondervan, especially Webb Younce, Dirk Buursma (for twenty-six years, Dirk and I have been doing this together!), and Alicia Kasen. Curtis Yates, Mike Salisbury, and Alli Sepulveda have been longtime supporters I pray I never have to do without.

Mary Kay Smith read an early manuscript of this book and made her usual helpful comments and then was joined by a number of Substack readers—some of whose quotes found their way into this manuscript, but all of whom are greatly appreciated for their gentle corrections and insights: Jeremiah Rittenhouse, Bill Walkup, Nancy Clameau, Dorothy Suskind, Bailey Russell, T. Braught, Doug Macrae, Neil DeSiato, Melva Buhrer, Laura Kates, Cheryl Ricker, Leah Holder Green, Nancy Halloran, Taylor Pitkins, Aurelie Magnuson, Vanessa Samuel, Jonathan Hefner, Sandy McKeown, Jay Dee, and Jennifer Connelly.

I also want to thank Cherry Hills Community Church, where I serve as a teaching pastor, and our senior pastor, Curt Taylor. I had the pleasure of preaching on many of these topics over the past few years, which ended up shaping the core of this book.

Finally, always Lisa, who has been on this journey with me for more than forty years now. Life is much better when we do it together.

# NOTES

## Introduction

1. William Law, *A Serious Call to a Devout and Holy Life* (Dutton, 1906), 218.
2. Law, *Serious Call*, 218–19.
3. Law, *Serious Call*, 351.
4. Karl Barth, *The Epistle to the Romans*, trans. Edwyn Hoskyns (Oxford University Press, 1933), 433.
5. John Stott, *Romans: God's Good News for the World* (InterVarsity, 1994), 322.

## Chapter 1: Dismantling Restlessness

1. Safiya Richardson et al., "Presenting Characteristics, Comorbidities, and Outcomes Among 5700 Patients Hospitalized with COVID-19 in the New York City Area," *JAMA* 323, no. 20 (2020): 2052–59, https://jamanetwork.com/journals/jama/fullarticle/2765184.
2. Henry Drummond, *Pax Vobiscum: An Address* (Hodder & Stoughton, 1890), 21.
3. John Calvin, *Institutes of the Christian Religion*, ed. John T. McNeill (Westminster, 1960), II.3.1, 40.
4. Drummond, *Pax Vobiscum*, 31.
5. Drummond, *Pax Vobiscum*, 32.
6. Jingjing Meng et al., "Prevalence of Hypochondriac Symptoms Among Health Science Students in China: A Systematic Review and Meta-analysis," *PLoS One* 14, no. 9 (2019), www.ncbi.nlm.nih.gov/pmc/articles/PMC6748570/.

7. Drummond, *Pax Vobiscum*, 36.

8. Drummond, *Pax Vobiscum*, 36–37.

## Chapter 2: Dismantling the Need to Be in Control

1. Brother Lawrence and Frank Laubach, *Practicing His Presence* (SeedSowers, 1973), 36.

2. R. Somerset Ward, *To Jerusalem: Devotional Studies in Mystical Religion* (1931; repr., Morehouse, 1994), 15.

3. Ward, *To Jerusalem*, 16.

4. From a sermon, based on Isaiah 52:4, preached by William Carey at a Northampton Baptist Association meeting in Nottingham, England, May 30, 1792; see "Deathless Sermon," Wikipedia, accessed April 16, 2025, https://en.wikipedia.org/wiki/Deathless_Sermon.

5. Ward, *To Jerusalem*, 16.

6. Ward, *To Jerusalem*, 17.

7. Ward, *To Jerusalem*, 139.

8. Ward, *To Jerusalem*, 17–18.

9. Ward, *To Jerusalem*, 18.

10. Ward, *To Jerusalem*, 18.

11. Dr. and Mrs. Howard Taylor, *Hudson Taylor's Spiritual Secret* (1989; repr., Moody, 2009).

12. Garth Lean, *Frank Buchman: On the Tail of a Comet* (Helmers & Howard, 1988).

13. Garth Lean, *Good God, It Works! An Experiment in Faith* (Blandford, 1974).

14. Brant Hansen, *Unoffendable: How Just One Change Can Make All of Life Better* (W Publishing, 2015), 190.

15. Hansen, *Unoffendable*, 190, italics in original.

## Chapter 3: Dismantling Family First

1. Richard Baxter, *A Christian Directory*, vol. 1 of *Christian Ethics* (R. Edwards, 1825), 109–10.

2. Thomas Smith, ed., *The Works of Thomas Brooks*, vol. 1 (J. Nichol, 1866), 391.

## Chapter 4: Dismantling Isolation

1. Stanley J. Grenz, "Theological Foundations for Male-Female Relationships," *Journal of the Evangelical Theological Society* 41, no. 4 (1998): 620, https://etsjets.org/wp-content/uploads/2010/06/files_JETS -PDFs_41_41-4_41-4-pp615-630-JETS.pdf.

2. Nate Larkin, *Samson and the Pirate Monks: Calling Men to Authentic Brotherhood* (Thomas Nelson, 2006), 67.

3. Larkin, *Samson and the Pirate Monks*, 68.

4. Larkin, *Samson and the Pirate Monks*, 68.

5. Watchman Nee, *Love Not the World: A Prophetic Call to Holy Living* (CLC Publications, 1968), 91.

6. Nee, *Love Not the World*, 94.

7. Nee, *Love Not the World*, 100.

8. Quoted in Liz Mineo, "Good Genes Are Nice, but Joy Is Better," *Harvard Gazette*, April 11, 2017, https://news.harvard.edu/gazette /story/2017/04/over-nearly-80-years-harvard-study-has-been-showing -how-to-live-a-healthy-and-happy-life/.

9. Mineo, "Good Genes Are Nice."

10. Mineo, "Good Genes Are Nice."

## Chapter 5: Dismantling Self-Centered Salvation

1. Cited in Greg McKeown, *Essentialism: The Disciplined Pursuit of Less* (Crown Business, 2014), 73–74.

2. C. S. Lewis, *The Screwtape Letters* (Spire, 1976), 119.

3. William Law, *A Serious Call to a Devout and Holy Life* (Dutton, 1909), 101.

## Chapter 6: Dismantling the Need for Comfort

1. William Gurnall, *The Christian in Complete Armor* (1845; repr., Verlag, 2024), 590.

2. J. I. Packer, *God's Plans for You* (Crossway, 2001), 119.

3. Gurnall, *Christian in Complete Armor*, 590.

4. Thomas Brooks, *The Mute Christian Under the Smarting Rod* (Reformed Church Publications, 2009), 11.

5. Thomas Brooks, "The Signal Presence of God with His People," in *The Complete Works of Thomas Brooks*, vol. 5, ed. Thomas Smith (J. Nichol, 1886), 491.

6. John Calvin, *Institutes of the Christian Religion*, ed. John T. McNeill (Westminster, 1960), III.8.1, 702.

7. Calvin, *Institutes*, III.8.1, 702.

8. Calvin, *Institutes*, III.8.1, 702.

9. Brooks, *Mute Christian*, 21.

10. See Brooks, *Mute Christian*, 25–26.

11. Brooks, *Mute Christian*, 48.

12. Brooks, *Mute Christian*, 120.

13. Brooks, *Mute Christian*, 22–23.

14. Brooks, *Mute Christian*, 23.

15. Thomas Brooks, *The Mute Christian Under the Smarting Rod*, in *The Complete Works of Thomas Brooks*, vol. 1, ed. Thomas Smith (J. Nichol, 1866), 397, italics in original.

16. Calvin, *Institutes*, III.8.2, 703.

17. Calvin, *Institutes*, III.8.3, 704.

18. Calvin, *Institutes*, III.8.5, 705–6.

19. Calvin, *Institutes*, III.8.6, 706.

20. Calvin, *Institutes*, III.8.7, 707–8.

21. Brooks, *Works*, vol. 1, 304.

22. Brooks, *Works*, vol. 1, 391.

23. Brooks, *Works*, vol. 5, 491.

## Chapter 7: Dismantling the Demand for a Sin-Free Life

1. Thomas Brooks, *The Mute Christian Under the Smarting Rod* (Reformed Church Publications, 2009), 123.

2. John Owen, *Of the Mortification of Sin in Believers*, in *Overcoming Sin and Temptation: Three Classic Works by John Owen*, ed. Kelly Kapic and Justin Taylor (Crossway, 2006), 86–89.

3. Owen, *Mortification of Sin*, 87.

4. Andrew A. Bonar, *Memoir and Remains of the Rev. Robert Murray M'Cheyne* (W. Middleton, 1852), 254.

5. Thomas Brooks, *Precious Remedies Against Satan's Devices*, device 1, remedy 6, Grace Gems, accessed April 2, 2025, www.gracegems.org /Brooks/precious_remedies_against_satan7.htm.

6. Brooks, *Precious Remedies*, device 8, remedy 2.

7. Richard Baxter, *A Christian Directory*, vol. 1 of *Christian Ethics* (R. Edwards, 1825), 256.

8. Thomas Brooks, *The Mute Christian Under the Smarting Rod*, in *The Complete Works of Thomas Brooks*, vol. 1, ed. Thomas Smith (J. Nichol, 1866), 367.

9. Brooks, *Mute Christian*, 368.

10. Brooks, *Mute Christian*, 369.

11. Brooks, *Mute Christian*, 369.

12. Brooks, *Mute Christian*, 369.

13. Milton Vincent, *A Gospel Primer for Christians: Learning to See the Glories of God's Love* (Focus Publishing, 2008), 31.

## Chapter 8: Dismantling Apathy Toward the Church

1. "Martyr Gorazd of Prague, Bohemia, and Moravo-Cilezsk," Orthodox Church of America, accessed April 4, 2025, www.oca.org/saints/lives/2017 /09/04/102375-martyr-gorazd-of-prague-bohemia-and-moravo-cilezsk.

2. Augustine, "Sermon 25: On the Words of the Gospel, Matthew 14:24," Christian Classics Ethereal Library, accessed April 4, 2025, www.ccel.org/ccel/schaff/npnf106/npnf106.vii.xxvii.html.

3. Bonnie Harvey, *D. L. Moody: The American Evangelist* (Barbour, 1997), 9.

4. J. B. Lightfoot, *Epistle to the Colossians* (Macmillan, 1875), 231, www .gutenberg.org/files/50857/50857-h/50857-h.htm, emphasis added.

5. John Deppen, "Hancock the Superb: Winfield Scott Hancock and the Battle of Gettysburg," *Warfare History Network*, April 2004, https:// warfarehistorynetwork.com/article/hancock-the-superb-winfield -scott-hancock-the-battle-of-gettysburg/.

## Chapter 9: Dismantling a Materialistic Worldview

1. Iain M. Duguid, *Daniel*, Reformed Expository Commentary (P&R, 2008), 185.

2. Duguid, *Daniel*, 187.

3. Duguid, *Daniel*, 188.

4. John Mark Comer, *God Has a Name* (Zondervan, 2017), 108–12.

5. John Peter Lange, *A Commentary on the Holy Scriptures: The Gospel According to Matthew* (Scribner, 1865), 325.

6. Cited in Wally Odum, "This Game Called Life," CBN, accessed April 5, 2025, https://cbn.com/devotions/game-called-life.

7. Shannon McIntyre, "Sheila Walsh Overcame Tortured Past After 'Angel' Brought Her a Lamb," God Reports, April 29, 2019, www .godreports.com/2019/04/sheila-walsh-overcame-tortured-past-after -angel-brought-her-a-lamb/.

## Chapter 10: Dismantling the Allure of Earthly Splendor

1. Liane Schmidt et al., "How Context Alters Value: The Brain's Valuation and Affective Regulation System Link Price Cues to Experienced Taste Pleasantness," *Scientific Reports* 7, no. 8098 (2017), www.nature.com/articles/s41598-017-08080-0; see David DiSalvo, "How Your Brain Makes You Think Expensive Wine Tastes Better," *Psychology Today*, September 8, 2017, www.psychologytoday.com /blog/neuronarrative/201709/how-your-brain-makes-you-think -expensive-wine-tastes-better.

2. Gabe Ulla, "The Hot New Heist: Would You Believe It's Stealing Wine?," *Town and Country*, November 30, 2023, www.townand countrymag.com/leisure/drinks/a45852344/wine-heist-crime-scandal -news/.

3. Juan Tello, Kerry Waddell, and Rüdiger Krech, eds., "Unrecorded Alcohol: What the Evidence Tells Us," World Health Organization, July 2, 2021, https://iris.who.int/bitstream/handle/10665/352516/9789240044463 -eng.pdf.

4. William Law, *A Serious Call to a Devout and Holy Life* (Dutton, 1906), 11–19, 56–65.

5. Mark Batterson, *All In: You Are One Decision Away from a Totally Different Life* (Zondervan, 2013), 62.

6. Christopher P. Niemiec, Richard M. Ryan, and Edward L. Deci,

"The Path Taken: Consequences of Attaining Intrinsic and Extrinsic Aspirations in Post-College Life," *Journal of Research in Personality* 43, no. 3 (June 2009): 291–306, www.sciencedirect.com/science/article /abs/pii/S0092656608001360.

7. Arthur C. Brooks, *From Strength to Strength: Finding Success, Happiness, and Deep Purpose in the Second Half of Life* (Penguin, 2022), 140.

8. Brooks, *From Strength to Strength*, 141.

9. Frederick William Faber, *All for Jesus: Or the Easy Ways of Divine Love* (Richardson, 1855), 2.

10. Rodney Reeves, *Spirituality According to John: Abiding in Christ in the Johannine Writings* (InterVarsity, 2021), 236, italics in original.

11. Reeves, *Spirituality According to John*, 236.

12. Reeves, *Spirituality According to John*, 237.

13. Reeves, *Spirituality According to John*, 238.

## Chapter 11: Dismantling a Sense of Entitlement

1. Jordan Potter, "The Absurd Story of Fyodor Dostoyevsky's Fake Execution," *Far Out*, March 17, 2024, https://faroutmagazine.co.uk /story-fyodor-dostoyevskys-fake-execution/.

2. John Calvin, *Institutes of the Christian Religion*, ed. John T. McNeill (Westminster, 1960), II.16.2, 505.

3. William Law, *A Serious Call to a Devout and Holy Life* (Dutton, 1906), 281–82.

## Chapter 12: Dismantling Complacent Ignorance

1. John Bevere, *The Fear of the Lord: Discover the Key to Intimately Knowing God*, rev. ed. (Charisma House, 2006), 127–28.

2. Peter D. Kaufman, ed., *Poor Charlie's Almanak: The Wit and Wisdom of Charles T. Munger*, rev. ed. (Stripe, 2023), 369.

3. Mike Woodruff, "The Good Friday Update" (weekly email), April 15, 2022.

4. William Gurnall, *The Christian in Complete Armor* (1845; repr., Verlag, 2024), 584.

5. Gurnall, *Christian in Complete Armor*, 584.

6. H. Newton Malony, "John Wesley and the Eighteenth Century Therapeutic Uses of Electricity," *Perspectives on Science and Christian Faith* 45 (December 1995): 244, www.asa3.org/ASA/PSCF/1995 /PSCF12-95Malony.html.

7. Hikaru Takeuchi et al., "The Impact of Television Viewing on Brain Structures: Cross-Sectional and Longitudinal Analyses," *Cerebral Cortex* 25, no. 5 (2015): 1188–97, https://pubmed.ncbi.nlm.nih.gov/24256892/.

8. Robert S. Wilson et al., "Life-Span Cognitive Activity, Neuropathologic Burden, and Cognitive Aging," *Neurology* 81, no. 4 (2013): 314–21, https://pubmed.ncbi.nlm.nih.gov/23825173/.

9. See "Reading 'Can Help Reduce Stress,'" *The Telegraph*, March 30, 2009, www.telegraph.co.uk/news/health/news/5070874/Reading-can -help-reduce-stress.html.

10. Charles Haddon Spurgeon, "Paul—His Cloak and His Books," sermon delivered on November 29, 1863, Spurgeon Center, accessed April 5, 2025, www.spurgeon.org/resource-library/sermons/paul-his -cloak-and-his-books/#flipbook/.

11. Chantal Da Silva, "Michelle Obama Tells a Secret: 'I Have Been at Every Powerful Table You Can Think of . . . They Are Not That Smart,'" *Newsweek*, December 4, 2018, www.newsweek.com/michelle -obama-tells-secret-i-have-been-every-powerful-table-you-can-think -1242695.

12. Charlie Munger, "USC School of Law Commencement Address," May 13, 2007, in *Poor Charlie's Almanak*, www.stripe.press/poor-charlies -almanack/talk-ten?

13. Charles Chu, "In the Time You Spend on Social Media Each Year, You Could Read 200 Books," Quartz, updated July 20, 2022, https:// qz.com/895101/in-the-time-you-spend-on-social-media-each-year -you-could-read-200-books; see also Philip Yancy, "The Death of Reading Is Threatening the Soul," *Washington Post*, July 21, 2017, www.washingtonpost.com/news/acts-of-faith/wp/2017/07/21/the -death-of-reading-is-threatening-the-soul/.

14. Dallas Willard, *Renovation of the Heart: Putting On the Character of Christ*, rev. ed. (NavPress, 2021), 107.

## Epilogue

1. C. E. B. Cranfield, *Romans* (T&T Clark, 1979), 607.
2. Cranfield, *Romans*, 608.
3. Cranfield, *Romans*, 608.
4. Gerrit Scott Dawson, *Jesus Ascended: The Meaning of Christ's Continuing Incarnation* (P&R, 2004), 170–71.
5. Fulton J. Sheen, *Way to Happiness* (Doubleday, 1954), 23.

# CONNECTING WITH
# GARY THOMAS

For more information about Gary's ministry,
check out his Substack page:
https://substack.com/@garythomasbooks

To view his website, including his upcoming
speaking engagements, go to:
www.garythomas.com

To invite Gary to speak at your church or
community event, please contact:
alli@garythomas.com